LATIN Grammar

ANSWER KEY

Second Edition
Revised and Expanded

Douglas Wilson
Karen Craig

Canon Press

MOSCOW, IDAHO

Douglas Wilson and Karen Craig, *Latin Grammar Book I (Answer Key)*

First Edition © 1992 by Douglas Wilson
Second Edition © 1997 by Douglas Wilson and Karen Craig

Published 1997 by Canon Press, P.O. Box 8741, Moscow, ID 83843
800-488-2034

Printed in the United States of America

ISBN: 1-885767-38-2

TABLE OF CONTENTS

EXERCISE ONE

A. The following is a list of Latin words you have not yet learned. The purpose of this exercise is pronunciation only. Next to each word, phonetically spell out how each word sounds in English. Do not concern yourself with the meanings of the words.

1.	agricolam	a GRI ko lahm
2.	poētae	po AY teye
3.	fēminās	FEY min ahs
4.	dōnum	DOH num
5.	dabant	DAH bant
6.	dabāmus	da BAH mus
7.	videō	WI de o
8.	vidēmus	wi DAY mus
9.	habent	HA bent
10.	rem	rem
11.	diēs	DI ays
12.	diēbus	di AY bus
13.	laudant	LAU dant
14.	manibus	MA ni bus
15.	īnsulārum	een su LAHR um
16.	gaudium	GOW di um
17.	nāvigāvit	nah wi GAH wit
18.	amīcus	a MEE cus
19.	vulnerō	WUL ner roh

EXERCISE TWO

A. Please answer the following questions about parts of speech.

1. What is a noun? *A noun is a person, place, or thing.*
2. Give three examples of English nouns. *Dog, house, John*
3. What is a verb? *A verb shows being or action.*
4. Give three examples of English verbs. *Sing, hit, run*
5. What is an adjective? *An adjective describes a noun.*
6. Give three examples of English adjectives. *Hot, red, large*
7. Give an example of an adjective replacing a noun. *The good love God.*
8. What is an adverb? *An adverb modifies a verb.*
9. Give three examples of English adverbs. *Well, swiftly, slowly*
10. What is a personal pronoun? *A word that stands in place of a personal name or names.*
11. Give three examples of English personal pronouns. *He, she, they*

EXERCISE THREE

A. Spell out in English how each Latin word should be pronounced and place the accent properly.

1. laudō	LAU doh
2. laudās	LAU dahs
3. laudat	LAU dat
4. laudāmus	lau DAH mus
5. laudātis	lau DAH tis
6. laudant	LAU dant

B. Chant the following paradigms ten times through.
[Teachers Note: It is helpful to chant the verb endings ATTACHED to a verb. It ensures accurate renderings of verb stems combined with the appropriate endings.]

ō, s, t! mus, tis, nt!

amō, amās, amat! amāmus, amātis, amant!

C. Translate the following English into Latin.
1. You (singular) praise. *Laudās.*
2. We preserve. *Conservāmus.*
3. She explores. *Explorat.*
4. He shouts. *Clamat.*
5. They love. *Amant.*
6. You (plural) praise. *Laudātis.*
7. I delay. *Tardō.*

D. Translate the following Latin into English.
1. Laudāmus. *We praise.*
2. Oppugnant. *They attack.*
3. Stātis. *You (pl.) stand.*
4. Portās. *You (s.) carry.*
5. Narrō. *I tell.*
6. Navigat. *He sails.*
7. Spectā! *Look! (singular)*
8. Amāte! *Love! (plural)*
9. Portāte! *Carry! (plural)*
10. Dā! *Give! (singular)*

E. List all the English words you can think of which come from this lesson's vocabulary words.
1. *Laud*—praise
2. *Laudable*—praiseworthy
3. *Laudatory*—containing praise

[Teachers note: these words actually come from the Latin *noun* for praise, which is *laus, laudis.*]

F. Answer the following questions.

1. What is a dipthong? *It is a combination of two vowels together to make a single sound.*
2. In Latin, what sound does *ae* make? *It makes the sound of "ai" as in "aisle", or of the word "eye"*
3. In Latin, what sound does *v* make? *It makes the sound of a "w".*
4. In words of two syllables, where does the accent fall? *On the first syllable.*
5. What is a noun? *It is a person, place or thing.*
6. What is a verb? *A verb shows being or action.*
7. List the six tenses we will study in this book. *Present, imperfect, future, perfect, pluperfect, and future perfect.*
8. To what time does the pluperfect tense refer? *The time past the past—he had praised.*
9. The pronoun *they* is associated with what person, and what number? *It is third person plural.*
10. How many endings are there for each tense? *There are six verb endings for each tense.*
11. What is the first person singular ending for First Conjugation verbs? *The ending is -ō.*
12. What is the third person plural ending for First Conjugation verbs? *The ending is -nt.*
13. What is the characteristic feature of First Conjugation verbs? *They all have "ā" at the end of the stem.*
14. How is the stem of First Conjugation verbs found? *It is found by dropping the -re from the second form of the verb.*
15. When a verb is looked up in a dictionary, how many forms of the verb will be seen? *There will be four forms.*

EXERCISE FOUR

A. Spell out in English how each Latin word should be pronounced and place the accent properly.

1. mundus		MUN dus
2. spectō		SPEK toh
3. Deus		DE us
4. portant		POR tant
5. puella		pu EL la
6. puellam		pu EL lam
7. Deum		DE um
8. amāmus		a MAH mus
9. puellās		pu EL lahs
10. laudātis		lou DAH tis

B. Chant each of the following paradigms ten times through.

[Teacher's Note: It is helpful to have the students practice several different nouns in chant form (*via, viae, viae, viam, viā, viae, viārum, viīs, viās, viīs*) to develop the habit of quickly declining a noun. This also ensures that students are accurately finding noun stems. For the chanting practices, one might choose to chant the verb endings five times, then conjugate five different verbs in chant form, next the noun endings five times, and finally decline five different nouns.]

ō, s, t! mus, tis, nt!
amō, amās, amat! amāmus, amātis, amant!
a, ae, ae, am, ā! ae, ārum, īs, ās, īs!
us, ī, ō, um, ō! ī, ōrum, īs, ōs, īs!
um, ī, ō, um, ō! a, ōrum, īs, a, īs!

C. Translate the following English into Latin.

[Teacher's Note: Present tense verbs may be translated in the simple declarative (*he loves*), the progressive (*he is loving*), or the emphatic (*he does love*) modes.]

1. The women praise God, but the poet does not love God. *Fēminae Deum laudant, sed poēta Deum nōn amat.*
2. The manservant is giving an example. *Famulus exemplum dat.*
3. He looks at the flame, but he does not condemn the son. *Flammam spectat, sed fīlium nōn damnat.*
4. Greed lives in the settler. *Avaritia incolam habitat.*
5. The messenger often calls the mob together. *Nuntius turbam saepe convocat.*
6. The girls are wandering and they approach the forest. *Puellae errant et silvam appropinquant.*
7. Rumor always disturbs the farmer. *Fāma agricolam semper agitat.*
8. The sailors explore the island. *Nautae insulam explorant.*
9. The cart does carry the women and the maidservants. *Carrus fēminās et famulās portat.*
10. We are praising God. *Deum laudāmus.*

D. Translate the following Latin into English.

1. Praemium copiās tardat. *The reward delays the troops.*
2. Agricolae nautās pugnant. *The farmers are fighting the sailors.*
3. Nautae prōvinciam explorant. *The sailors explore the province.*
4. Puella Deum appropinquat. *The girl approaches God.*
5. Incola silvam habitat. *The settler lives in the forest.*
6. Servī saepe dominōs nōn pugnant. *The slaves do not often fight the masters.*
7. Vestigia periculum dēmōnstrant. *The footprints point out the danger.*
8. Argentum fīlium conciliat. *The money wins over the son.*
9. Discipulus dominum spectat. *The student watches (looks at) the master.*
10. Fēmina comam conservat. *The woman saves the hair.*

E. List all the English words you can think of which come from the vocabulary learned thus far.

1. Deity
2. Deist
3. divination
4. divine
5. divinity
6. amateur
7. amiable
8. amity
9. enamoured
10. enemy

F. Answer the following questions.

    1. How many cases are there for Latin nouns? *There are five cases.*

    2. To what time does the pluperfect tense refer? *It refers to the time past the past—he had sung.*

    3. How is a *v* pronounced? *It is pronounced as a "w."*

    4. What are the suffixes on the end of Latin nouns called? *They are called case endings.*

    5. What is the accusative plural ending for the First Declension? *The ending is -ās.*

    6. Does word order determine grammatical function in Latin? *No.*

    7. What is the genitive singular ending for the First Declension? *The ending is -ae.*

    8. How many cases are there for each noun? *There are five cases.*

    9. What are the names of these cases? *Nominative, genitive, dative, accusative, and ablative.*

    10. How many genders are there for Latin nouns? *There are three genders.*

Exercise Five–A

A. Spell out in English how each Latin word should be pronounced and place the accent properly.

1. laudābāmus	lau dah BAH mus
2. laudābant	lau DAH bant
3. vocābant	wo KAH bant
4. vocant	WO kant
5. amābāmus	a mah BAH mus
6. amābimus	a MAH bi mus
7. laudābunt	lau DAH bunt
8. spectābunt	spek TAH bunt
9. spectō	SPEK toh
10. vocābit	wo KAH bit

B. Chant each of the following paradigms ten times through.

    ō, s, t! mus, tis, nt!

    amō, amās, amat! amāmus, amātis, amant!

    a, ae, ae, am, ā! ae, ārum, īs, ās, īs!

    us, ī, ō, um, ō! ī, ōrum, īs, ōs, īs!

    um, ī, ō, um, ō! a, ōrum, īs, a, īs!

    bam, bās, bat! bāmus, bātis, bant!

    bō, bis, bit! bimus, bitis, bunt!

C. Translate the following review sentences.

    1. Deus mundum amat. *God loves the world.*

    2. Puellam amat. *He loves the girl.*

    3. Puella amat. *The girl loves.*

    4. Spectāmus. *We look at (watch).*

5. Amātis. *You (plural) love.*
6. Vocant. *They call.*
7. Vocant puellam. *They call the girl.*
8. Puella vocat. *The girl calls.*
9. Puella Deum appropinquat. *The girl approaches God.*
10. Vocō. *I call.*

D. Translate the following English into Latin.

1. They were praising and loving God. *Deum laudābant et amābant.*
2. I shall always praise God. *Deum semper laudābō.*
3. God was watching the world. *Deus mundum spectābat.*
4. The girl and the maid were often was praising God. *Puella et famula saepe Deum laudābat.*
5. The master will call. *Dominus vocābit.*
6. The girls will wander. *Puellae errābunt.*
7. They were shouting the reports. *Famās clamābant.*
8. The woman was not carrying the dish. *Fēmina patellam nōn portābat.*
9. You (pl.) were sailing. *Navigābātis.*
10. You (sing.) will not wound the son. *Fīlium nōn vulnerās.*

E. Translate the following Latin into English.

1. Laudābimus. *We shall praise.*
2. Puellam rogābunt. *They will ask the girl.*
3. Puella mutābit. *The girl will change.*
4. Deus amābat. *God was loving.*
5. Deum amābat. *He was loving God.*
6. Famulī stant. *The male servants are standing.*
7. Dominōs narrant. *They tell the masters.*
8. Deum laudābātis. *You (pl.) used to praise (were praising) God.*
9. Rotam portābitis. *You (pl.) will carry the wheel.*
10. Puellās nōn spectābāmus. *We were not watching (looking at) the girls.*

F. Answer the following questions.

1. In Latin, what sound does an *ae* make? *It sounds like "ai" in "aisle", or like "eye".*
2. In words of two syllables, where does the accent fall? *It falls on the first syllable.*
3. To what time does the perfect tense refer? *It refers to completed action in the past.*
4. How many endings are there for each tense of a Latin verb? *There are six endings for each tense.*
5. How many declensions are there for Latin nouns? *There are five declensions.*
6. What is the second person singular, imperfect tense ending for *spectō*? *The ending is -bās.*
7. What is the first person plural, future tense ending for *vocō*? *The ending is -bimus.*
8. What is the first person singular, imperfect tense ending for *amō*? *The ending is -bam.*
9. What is the third person singular, imperfect tense ending for *dō*? *The ending is -bat.*
10. What is the third person plural, future tense ending for *portō*? *The ending is -bunt.*

Exercise Five–b

A. Spell out in English how each Latin word should be pronounced and place the accent properly.

1. agricola	a GRI ko la
2. agricolam	a GRI ko lam
3. poēta	po AY ta
4. poētās	po AY tahs
5. viārum	wi AH rum
6. discipulōrum	dis kip u LOH rum
7. nūntius	NOON ti us
8. nūntiō	NOON ti oh
9. gladium	GLAD i um
10. gladiōs	GLAD i ohs

B. Chant each of the following paradigms ten times through.

ō, s, t! mus, tis, nt!
amō, amās, amat! amāmus, amātis, amant!
a, ae, ae, am, ā! ae, ārum, īs, ās, īs!
us, ī, ō, um, ō! ī, ōrum, īs, ōs, īs!
um, ī, ō, um, ō! a, ōrum, īs, a, īs!
bam, bās, bat! bāmus, bātis, bant!
bō, bis, bit! bimus, bitis, bunt!

C. Translate the following review sentences.
　1. Poēta Deum laudābit. *The poet will praise God.*
　2. Fēminae Deum laudābant. *The women were praising God.*
　3. Nautae vocant. *The sailors call.*
　4. Fēminae nautam vocant. *The women call the sailor.*
　5. Poētae puellās amābant. *The poets were loving the girls.*
　6. Poēta et agricola Deum laudābant. *The poet and farmer were praising God.*
　7. Nauta et puella fēminam spectant. *The sailor and girl look at the woman.*
　8. Nautae puellam portant. *The sailors carry the girl.*
　9. Agricola puellam spectat. *The farmer looks at the girl.*
　10. Puellās nōn spectābāmus. *We were not looking at the girls.*

D. Translate the following English into Latin.
　1. The farmers call. *Agricolae vocant.*
　2. The farmer was calling. *Agricola vocābat.*
　3. The farmers will call. *Agricolae vocābunt.*
　4. They will call the farmers. *Agricolās vocābunt.*
　5. They will call the woman. *Fēminam vocābunt.*
　6. They were calling the women. *Fēminās vocābant.*

7. The sailor carries. *Nauta portat.*
8. The poet will love the woman. *Poēta fēminam amābit.*
9. The woman looks at the road. *Fēmina viam spectat.*
10. The women will look at the road. *Fēminae viam spectābunt.*
11. The flames were ravaging the province. *Flammae prōvinciam vexābant.*
12. The maid approaches the window, but the window will not change.
   Famula fenestram appropinquat, sed fenestra nōn mutābit.
13. The farmer labors to change the wall. *Agricola vallum mutāre laborat.*
14. The sailors were calling the winds. *Nautae ventōs vocābant.*
15. The poet will not tell the rumor. *Poēta fāmam nōn narrābit.*

E. Translate the following Latin into English.

1. Poētae puellās amābant. *The poets were loving the girls.*
2. Poēta Deum laudābit. *The poet will praise God.*
3. Nautae vocant. *The sailors call.*
4. Fēminae nautam vocant. *The women call the sailor.*
5. Fēminae Deum laudābant. *The women were praising God.*
6. Agricolae viam spectant. *The farmers look at the road.*
7. Agricola puellam spectat. *The farmer looks at the girl.*
8. Nautae puellam portant. *The sailors carry the girl.*
9. Nauta et puella fēminam spectant. *The sailor and girl look at the woman.*
10. Poēta et agricola Deum laudābant. *The poet and farmer were praising God.*
11. Fīlius fluvium dēmōnstrābat. *The son was pointing out the river.*
12. Līberī ludōs postulant. *The children demand games.*
13. Sociī nuntiōs nōn pugnābant. *The friends were not fighting the messengers.*
14. Populī scopulum habitant. *The people do live in the rock formation.*
15. Gladium nōn dās. *You (s.) do not give the sword.*

F. List all the English words you can think of which come from recently studied Latin vocabulary words.

> [Teacher's Note: The student will find it helpful to check some of his own words by looking them up in the dictionary. This would be an appropriate time to teach this skill. It will be interesting to note which words are derived from nouns and which ones from verbs.]

G. Answer the following questions.

1. To what time does the pluperfect tense refer? *It refers to the time past the past—they had run.*
2. How many endings are there for each tense of a Latin verb? *There are six endings for each tense.*
3. How many case endings are there for each declension of a Latin noun? *There are ten case endings for each Latin noun.*
4. What is the third person singular ending, future tense for *spectō*? *The ending is -bit.*

5. What is the second person plural ending, imperfect tense for *vocō*? *The ending is* -bātis.
6. Why is it important to learn the genitive singular ending for nouns? *The genitive singular ending shows to which declension a noun belongs.*
7. What gender is not found in the Second Declension? *The feminine gender is not found in the Second Declension.*
8. With neuter nouns, which case endings are always the same as one another? *The nominative singular and accusative singular endings are the same, and the nominative plural and accusative plural endings are the same.*
9. What words have you learned which will not change their endings? *The adverbs* saepe, non, semper, *and* cūr, *and the conjuctions* et *and* sed *do not change their endings.*
10. What does *saepe* mean? *It means* often.

EXERCISE SIX

A. Spell out in English how each Latin word should be pronounced and place the accent properly.

1. sum	sum
2. es	es
3. sunt	sunt
4. sumus	SU mus
5. eram	E ram
6. erat	E rat
7. erātis	e RAH tis
8. erō	E roh
9. erunt	E runt
10. eritis	e RI tis

B. Chant each of the following paradigms ten times through.

ō, s, t! mus, tis, nt!
amō, amās, amat! amāmus, amātis, amant!
a, ae, ae, am, ā! ae, ārum, īs, ās, īs!
us, ī, ō, um, ō! ī, ōrum, īs, ōs, īs!
um, ī, ō, um, ō! a, ōrum, īs, a, īs!
bam, bās, bat! bāmus, bātis, bant!
bō, bis, bit! bimus, bitis, bunt!
sum, es, est! sumus, estis, sunt!
eram, erās, erat! erāmus, erātis, erant!
erō, eris, erit! erimus, eritis, erunt!

C. Translate the following review sentences.

1. Fīlius fluvium dēmōnstrābat. *The son was pointing out the river.*
2. Līberī ludōvs postulant. *The children demand games.*
3. Sociī nuntiōs nōn pugnābant. *The friends were not fighting the messengers.*
4. Fēminae nautam vocant. *The women are calling the sailor.*
5. Poētae puellās amābant. *The poets used to love the girls.*
6. Poēta et agricola Deum laudābant. *The poet and the farmer were praising God.*
7. Nauta et puella fēminam spectant. *The sailor and the girl are watching the woman.*
8. Nautae puellam portant. *The sailors carry the girl.*
9. Nauta et puella incolās convocant. *The sailor and the girl call together the inhabitants.*
10. Fabulās narrant. *They tell the stories.*

D. Translate the following English into Latin.

1. You all were. *Erātis.*
2. He was. *Erat.*
3. I am. *Sum.*
4. We shall be. *Erimus.*
5. We were. *Erāmus.*
6. You are. *Es.*
7. You all are. *Estis.*
8. She will be. *Erit.*
9. It was. *Erat.*
10. They are. *Sunt.*

E. Translate the following Latin into English.

1. Nauta est. *He is a sailor.*
2. Nautae sunt. *They are sailors.*
3. Poēta es. *You are a poet.*
4. Poētae estis. *You are poets.*
5. Agricola sum. *I am a farmer.*
6. Agricolae sumus. *We are farmers.*
7. Dōnum est. *It is a gift.*
8. Vīnum est. *It is wine.*
9. Agricolae nōn sumus. *We are not farmers.*
10. Nauta nōn est. *He is not a sailor.*

F. Answer the following questions.

1. How many tenses have you learned for the verb of being? *Three.*
2. What does it mean to say a verb is irregular? *It means that it deviates from the pattern of other verbs.*
3. What is the third person singular, imperfect tense for *laudō*? *The ending is* -bat.
4. What is the third person singular, imperfect tense for *sum*? *It is* "erat."

5. What is the first person plural, future tense for *sum*? *It is "erimus."*
6. What gender usually fits First Declension nouns? *Feminine.*
7. How many declensions are there? *There are five.*
8. How many genders are there for Latin Nouns? *Three—masculine, feminine, and neuter.*
8. When translating a Latin sentence, what should you look for first? *Look first for the verb.*
9. To what time does the perfect tense refer? *It refers to completed action in the past.*

Exercise Seven

A. Spell out in English how each Latin word should be pronounced and place the accent properly.

1. laudāvī	lau DAH wee
2. laudāvistī	lau DAH wis tee
3. laudāvit	lau DAH wit
4. laudāvimus	lau DAH wi mus
5. laudāvistis	lau DAH wis tis
6. laudāvērunt	lau dah WAY runt
7. spectāvī	spek TAH wee
8. spectāvistī	spek TAH wis tee
9. spectāvit	spek TAH wit
10. spectāvimus	spek TAH wi mus

B. Chant each of the following paradigms ten times through.

ō, s, t! mus, tis, nt!
amō, amās, amat! amāmus, amātis, amant!
a, ae, ae, am, ā! ae, ārum, īs, ās, īs!
us, ī, ō, um, ō! ī, ōrum, īs, ōs, īs!
um, ī, ō, um, ō! a, ōrum, īs, a, īs!
bam, bās, bat! bāmus, bātis, bant!
bō, bis, bit! bimus, bitis, bunt!
sum, es, est! sumus, estis, sunt!
eram, erās, erat! erāmus, erātis, erant!
erō, eris, erit! erimus, eritis, erunt!
ī, istī, it! imus, istis, ērunt!

> [Teacher's Note: Now that the students have started to learn the principal parts of the verbs they learn, it will be a good idea to have them chant repeatedly the four principal parts for each new verb.]

C. Translate the following review sentences.

1. Fēmina et puella spectant viam. *The woman and girl look at the road.*
2. Poēta Deum laudābit. *The poet will praise God.*
3. Agricola puellam appropinquat. *The farmer approaches the girl.*

4. Deus amābat. *God was loving.*

5. Poēta et agricola equum agitābant. *The poet and farmer were driving the horse.*

6. Nauta et puella fēminam accusant. *The sailor and girl accuse the woman.*

7. Incolae viam dēmōnstrant. *The settlers point out the road.*

8. Vīnum spectant. *They look at the wine.*

9. Dōnum dat. *He gives the gift.*

10. Dōminī cōnsilium dant. *The lords give advice.*

D. Translate the following English into Latin.

1. You looked at the girl. *Puellam spectāvistī.*

2. The poet vexed the throng. *Poēta turbam vexāvit.*

3. The woman and the maidservant praised God. *Fēmina et famula Deum laudāvērunt.*

4. God loved the world. *Deus mundum amāvit.*

5. The slave carried the sword. *Servus gladium portāvit.*

6. The women delayed the advice. *Fēminae cōnsilium tardāvērunt.*

7. I explored the cave. *Antrum explorāvī.*

8. The friends carried the gifts. *Sociī dōna portāvērunt.*

9. We praised the wine. *Vīnum laudāvimus.*

10. You (pl.) looked at the swords. *Gladiōs spectāvistis.*

E. Translate the following Latin into English.

1. Spectāvistis. *You (plural) looked.*

2. Deum laudāvistis. *You (plural) praised God.*

3. Deum amāvistis. *You (plural) loved God.*

4. Deus amāvit. *God loved.*

5. Deus mundum amāvit. *God loved the world.*

6. Portāvērunt. *They carried.*

7. Gladiōs portāvērunt. *They carried the swords.*

8. Cōnsilium dedērunt. *They gave advice.*

9. Cōnsilium dedit. *He gave advice.*

10. Fēminae et puellae vocāvērunt. *The women and girls called.*

F. Answer the following questions.

1. How many declensions are there for Latin nouns? *There are five.*

2. How many conjugations are there for Latin verbs? *There are four.*

3. How many case endings are there for Latin nouns? *There are ten case endings.*

4. How many tenses will we study for Latin verbs? *We will study six.*

5. What are these tenses? *Present, imperfect, future, perfect, pluperfect, and future perfect.*

6. What is the third person plural, perfect tense for *vocō*? *It is "vocāvērunt."*

7. What is the first person singular, perfect tense for *amō*? *It is "amāvī."*

8. What is the second person plural, perfect tense for *spectō*? *It is "spectāvistis."*

9. What is the second person singular, perfect tense for *laudō*? *It is "laudāvistī."*

10. What is the third person singular, perfect tense for *portō*? *It is "portāvit."*

EXERCISE EIGHT

A. Spell out in English how each Latin word should be pronounced and place the accent properly.

1. laudāveram	lau DAH we ram
2. laudāverās	lau DAH we rahs
3. laudāverat	lau DAH we rat
4. laudāverāmus	lau dah we RAH mus
5. laudāverātis	lau dah we RAH tis
6. laudāverant	lau DAH we rant
7. spectāverō	spek TAH we roh
8. spectāveris	spek TAH we ris
9. spectāverit	spek TAH we rit
10. spectāverimus	spek tah WE ri mus

B. Chant each of the following paradigms ten times through.

ō, s, t! mus, tis, nt!

bam, bās, bat! bāmus, bātis, bant!

bō, bis, bit! bimus, bitis, bunt!

a, ae, ae, am, ā! ae, ārum, īs, ās, īs!

us, ī, ō, um, ō! ī, ōrum, īs, ōs, īs!

um, ī, ō, um, ō! a, ōrum, īs, a, īs!

sum, es, est! sumus, estis, sunt!

eram, erās, erat! erāmus, erātis, erant!

erō, eris, erit! erimus, eritis, erunt!

ī, istī, it! imus, istis, ērunt!

eram, erās, erat! erāmus, erātis, erant!

erō, eris, erit! erimus, eritis, erint!

C. Translate the following review sentences.

1. Fēmina spectat viam. *The woman looks at the road.*
2. Poēta laudābit. *The poet will praise.*
3. Agricola gladiōs dēmōnstrat. *The farmer shows the swords.*
4. Deus amābat mundum. *God was loving the world.*
5. Equī campum explorābant. *The horses explore the plain.*
6. Nauta et puella fēminās convocābant. *The sailor and girl were calling together the women.*
7. Famulus praemium mandat. *The manservant entrusts the prize.*
8. Vīnum portant. *They carry the wine.*
9. Equus agricolam vexat. *The horse vexes the farmer.*
10. Dōminī cōnsilium dant. *The masters give advice.*

D. Translate the following English into Latin.

    1. You had looked at the girl. *Puellam spectāverās.*

    2. The girl will have looked at the poet. *Puella poētam spectāverit.*

    3. The woman and the girl had praised God. *Fēmina et puella Deum laudāverant.*

    4. God had loved the world. *Deus mundum amāverat.*

    5. The woman will have given the sword. *Fēmina gladium dederit.*

    6. The women had given advice. *Fēminae cōnsilium dederant.*

    7. I shall have praised the advice. *Cōnsilium laudāverō.*

    8. We shall have carried the gifts. *Dōna portāverimus.*

    9. We had praised the wine. *Vīnum laudāverāmus.*

    10. You (pl.) will have looked at the swords. *Gladiōs spectāveritis.*

E. Translate the following Latin into English.

    1. Spectāveram. *I had looked.*

    2. Deum laudāverātis. *You (plural) had praised God.*

    3. Deum amāverō. *I shall have loved God.*

    4. Deus amāverat. *God had loved.*

    5. Deus mundum amāverat. *God had loved the world.*

    6. Portāverant. *They had carried.*

    7. Gladiōs portāverant. *They had carried the swords.*

    8. Cōnsilium dederat. *He had given advice.*

    9. Cōnsilium dederit. *He will have given advice.*

    10. Fēminae et puellae vocāverint. *The women and girls will have called.*

F. Answer the following questions.

    1. What is the genitive singular case ending for the First Declension? *The ending is -ae.*

    2. What is the gentive singular case ending for the Second Declension? *The ending is -ī.*

    3. What is the genitive singular case ending for the Second Declension neuter? *The ending is -ī.*

    4. To what time does the pluperfect tense refer? *It refers to a time past the past.*

    5. To what time does the future perfect tense refer? *It refers to a time past the future.*

    6. What is the third person plural, pluperfect tense for *vocō*? *It is "vocāverant."*

    7. What is the first person singular, future perfect tense for *amō*? *It is "amāverō."*

    8. What is the second person plural, pluperfect tense for *spectō*? *It is "spectāverātis."*

    9. What is the second person singular, future perfect tense for *laudō*? *It is "laudāveris."*

    10. What is the third person singular, pluperfect tense for *portō*? *It is "portāverat."*

EXERCISE NINE

A. Spell out in English how each Latin word should be pronounced and place the accent properly.

1. vocāveram	wo KAH we ram
2. vocāverās	wo KAH we rahs
3. vocāverat	wo KAH we rat
4. vocāverāmus	wo kah we RAH mus
5. vocāverātis	wo kah we RAH tis
6. vocāverant	wo KAH we rant
7. amāverō	a MAH we roh
8. amāveris	a MAH we ris
9. amāverit	a MAH we rit
10. amāverimus	a mah WE ri mus

B. Chant each of the following paradigms ten times through.

ō, s, t! mus, tis, nt!
bam, bās, bat! bāmus, bātis, bant!
bō, bis, bit! bimus, bitis, bunt!
a, ae, ae, am, ā! ae, ārum, īs, ās, īs!
us, ī, ō, um, ō! ī, ōrum, īs, ōs, īs!
um, ī, ō, um, ō! a, ōrum, īs, a, īs!
sum, es, est! sumus, estis, sunt!
eram, erās, erat! erāmus, erātis, erant!
erō, eris, erit! erimus, eritis, erunt!
ī, istī, it! imus, istis, ērunt!
eram, erās, erat! erāmus, erātis, erant!
erō, eris, erit! erimus, eritis, erint!

C. Translate the following review sentences.

1. Fīlius fluvium dēmōnstrābat. *The son was pointing out the river.*
2. Līberī ludōs postulant. *The children demand games.*
3. Sociī nuntiōs nōn pugnābant. *The friends were not fighting the messengers.*
4. Fēminae nautam vocant. *The women are calling the sailor.*
5. Poētae puellās amābant. *The poets used to love the girls.*
6. Nauta et puella fēminam accusant. *The sailor and the girl accuse the woman.*
7. Incolae viam dēmōnstrant. *The inhabitants show the way.*
8. Vīnum spectant. *They look at the wine.*
9. Dōnum dat. *He gives a gift.*
10. Dōminī cōnsilium dant. *The masters give advice.*

D. Translate the following English into Latin.

    1. Had you looked at the girl? *Spectāverāsne puellam?*

    2. Did the girl look at the poet? *Spectāvitne puella poētam?*

    3. Do the woman and the girl praise God? *Laudantne fēmina et puella Deum?*

    4. Will God love the world? *Amābitne Deus mundum?*

    5. Was the woman giving the sword? *Dābatne fēmina gladium?*

    6. Had the women given advice? *Dederantne fēminae cōnsilium?*

    7. Shall we have praised the advice? *Laudāverimusne cōnsilium?*

    8. You will have carried the gifts, will you not? *Nōnne dōna portāveris?*

    9. They had not praised the wine, had they? *Num vīnum laudāverant?*

    10. You (pl.) looked at the swords, didn't you? *Nōnne spectāvistis gladiōs?*

E. Translate the following Latin into English.

    1. Spectāveramne? *Had I looked?*

    2. Laudāverātisne Deum? *Had you (plural) praised God?*

    3. Amāverōne Deum? *Shall I have loved God?*

    4. Amāveratne Deus? *Had God loved?*

    5. Amāveratne Deus mundum? *Had God loved the world?*

    6. Nōnne spectat? *He looks, doesn't he?*

    7. Num laudātis? *You (plural) don't praise, do you?*

    8. Nōnne dederat cōnsilium? *He had given advice, hadn't he?*

    9. Num dederit cōnsilium? *He will not have given advice, will he?*

    10. Vocāverintne fēminae et puellae? *Will the women and girls have called?*

F. Answer the following questions.

    1. What is the genitive singular case ending for the Second Declension? *The ending is -ī.*

    2. To what time does the imperfect tense refer? *It refers to continuous time in the past.*

    3. Why is the genitive singular ending always listed with a noun in the dictionary? *It enables you to determine what declension the noun belongs to.*

    4. What is the principal gender for the First Declension? *The principal gender is feminine.*

    5. What suffix is attached to a word to turn a sentence into a question? *The suffix is -ne.*

    6. To which word is it attached? *It is attached to the first word in the sentence, which is usually the verb.*

    7. What word is used to create a question expecting a *no* for an answer? *The word is "num."*

    8. What word is used to create a question expecting a *yes* for an answer? *The word is "nōnne."*

    9. Where are these words placed in the sentence? *They are placed first in the sentence.*

    10. What is the third person singular, pluperfect tense, in a question for *portō*? *The word would be "portāveratne."*

Exercise Ten

A. Spell out in English how each Latin word should be pronounced and place the accent properly.

1. portāvit	por TAH wit
2. portāvimus	por TAH wi mus
3. portāvī	por TAH wee
4. portant	POR tant
5. portat	POR tat
6. portāmus	por TAH mus
7. portābunt	por TAH bunt
8. portābit	por TAH bit
9. portābimus	por TAH bi mus
10. portāveram	por TAH we ram

B. Chant each of the following paradigms ten times through.

ō, s, t! mus, tis, nt!

bam, bās, bat! bāmus, bātis, bant!

bō, bis, bit! bimus, bitis, bunt!

a, ae, ae, am, ā! ae, ārum, īs, ās, īs!

us, ī, ō, um, ō! ī, ōrum, īs, ōs, īs!

um, ī, ō, um, ō! a, ōrum, īs, a, īs!

sum, es, est! sumus, estis, sunt!

eram, erās, erat! erāmus, erātis, erant!

erō, eris, erit! erimus, eritis, erunt!

ī, istī, it! imus, istis, ērunt!

eram, erās, erat! erāmus, erātis, erant!

erō, eris, erit! erimus, eritis, erint!

C. Translate the following review sentences.

1. Mundum Deus amat. *God loves the world.*
2. Spectant. *They look at, watch.*
3. Puellam laudābunt. *They will praise the girl.*
4. Poētae puellās amābant. *The poets were loving the girls.*
5. Deus Fīlium dat. *God gives the Son.*
6. Fīlius Deum amat. *The Son loves God.*
7. Poētae estis. *You are poets.*
8. Vīnum est. *It is wine.*
9. Amāte! *Love!*
10. Cōnsilium dedērunt. *They have given advice.*
11. Portāverant. *They had carried.*
12. Gladiōs portāverant. *They had carried the swords.*

13. Cōnsilium dederat. *He had given advice.*
14. Cōnsilium dederit. *He will have given advice.*
15. Fēminae et puellae vocāverint. *The women and girls will have called.*

D. Translate the following English into Latin.
1. Christ is God. *Christus Deus est.*
2. Christ praises God. *Christus Deum laudat.*
3. The poet is a sailor. *Poēta est nauta.*
4. The sailor is a poet. *Nauta est poēta.*
5. The farmer calls the poet. *Agricola poētam vocat.*
6. The settler is a farmer. *Incola est agricola.*
7. The settler, a farmer, praises the decision. *Incola, agricola, sentientiam laudat.*
8. The sailor, a poet, praises the farmer. *Nauta, poēta, agricolam laudat.*
9. The farmers, poets, look at the road. *Agricolae, poētae, viam spectant.*
10. The farmers are poets. *Agricolae poētae sunt.*

E. Translate the following Latin into English.
1. Fēminae, poētae, Deum amābant. *The women, poets, were loving God.*
2. Fēmina, poēta, Deum amāvit. *The woman, a poet, loved God.*
3. Puella fēmina est. *The girl is a woman.*
4. Fēmina est. *She is a woman.*
5. Sunt fēminae. *They are women.*
6. Fēmina, poēta, agricolam spectāvit. *The woman, a poet, looked at the farmer.*
7. Spectāvimus fēminam, poētam. *We looked at the woman, a poet.*
8. Agricolae sunt. *They are farmers.*
9. Puellae fēminae sunt. *The girls are women.*
10. Agricolae nautae nōn sunt. *The farmers are not sailors.*

F. Answer the following questions.
1. What gender is not found in the Second Declension? *Feminine.*
2. To what time does the present tense refer? *Right now.*
3. What is the third person singular ending, future tense for *spectō*? *The ending is* -bit.
4. How many endings are there for each tense of a Latin verb? *There are six endings.*
5. In words of three syllables, where does the accent fall? *The accent falls on the second or third syllable from the end, depending on whether the vowel in the next to last syllable is long or short.*
6. What is apposition? *Apposition is when a noun is placed alongside another noun to explain it in greater detail.*
7. What is the predicate nominative? *It is when a noun in the predicate takes the nominative case because the verb is sum.*
8. Give an example of the predicate nominative in English. *This is he.*
9. Give an example of the predicate nominative in Latin. *Puella est fēmina.*
10. What mathematics sign does the verb *is* resemble? *The equal sign.*

EXERCISE ELEVEN

A. Spell out in English how each Latin word should be pronounced and place the accent properly.

1. agricolārum	a gri ko LAHR um
2. fīliōrum	fee li OH rum
3. poētae	po AY teye
4. fēminae	FAY min eye
5. fēminārum	fay min AH rum
6. servīs	SER wees
7. Deō	DE oh
8. deīs	DE ees
9. puellae	pu EL leye
10. poētīs	poh AY tees

B. Chant each of the following paradigms ten times through.

ō, s, t! mus, tis, nt!
bam, bās, bat! bāmus, bātis, bant!
bō, bis, bit! bimus, bitis, bunt!
a, ae, ae, am, ā! ae, ārum, īs, ās, īs!
us, ī, ō, um, ō! ī, ōrum, īs, ōs, īs!
um, ī, ō, um, ō! a, ōrum, īs, a, īs!
sum, es, est! sumus, estis, sunt!
eram, erās, erat! erāmus, erātis, erant!
erō, eris, erit! erimus, eritis, erunt!
ī, istī, it! imus, istis, ērunt!
eram, erās, erat! erāmus, erātis, erant!
erō, eris, erit! erimus, eritis, erint!

C. Translate the following review sentences.

1. Fēminās spectābant. *They were looking at the women.*
2. Poēta laudābit. *The poet will praise.*
3. Fēmina spectābit. *The woman will look at, will watch.*
4. Agricola et fēmina puellās laudāvērunt. *The farmer and woman praised the girls.*
5. Puellae et fēminae agricolam laudāverint. *The girls and women will have praised the farmer.*
6. Nauta et puella navigābant. *The sailor and the girl were sailing.*
7. Laudāte! *Praise!*
8. Dā! *Give!*
9. Nautae puellam amābant. *The sailors were loving the girl.*
10. Amāmus. *We love.*

D. Translate the following English into Latin.

1. The son of the sailor praises God. *Fīlius nautae Deum laudat.*
2. God loved the son of the maidservant. *Deus fīlium famulae amāvit.*
3. The poet's life was praising God. *Vīta nautae Deum laudābat.*
4. The Son of God carries the farmer's cares. *Fīlius Deī curās agricolae portat.*
5. The son of the woman looks at the window of the farmhouse. *Fīlius fēminae fenestram villae spectat.*
6. The woman's son gives the farmer a gift. *Fīlius fēminae agricolō dōnum dat.*
7. The woman's son tells the son of the farmer a legend. *Fīlius fēminae fīliō agricolae fabulam narrat.*
8. The farmer's son gives the woman's son a sword. *Fīlius agricolae fīliō fēminae gladium dat.*
9. The woman's slaves give the son the sword. *Servī fēminae gladium fīliō dant.*
10. The slaves of the women were showing the girl a garden. *Servī fēminārum puellae hortum dēmōnstrābant.*

E. Translate the following Latin into English.

1. Servī fēminārum puellās spectant. *The slaves of the women look at the girls.*
2. Fīlius agricolae dōnum dat. *The son of the farmer gives a gift.*
3. Fīlium fēminae spectō. *I look at the son of the woman.*
4. Servus agricolae fīlium agricolae spectāvit. *The slave of the farmer looked at the son of the farmer.*
5. Servum agricolae laudāverās. *You had praised the slave of the farmer.*
6. Dantne agricolae gladium fīliō? *Will the farmers give the sword to the son?* OR *Will they give the sword to the son of the farmer?*
7. Fēmina et puella agricolīs dōnum dant. *The woman and the girl give the gift to the farmers.*
8. Servus agricolae gladium fīliō agricolae dabit. *The farmer's slave will give a sword to the farmer's son.*
9. Praemium servō dabitis. *You will give a reward to the slave.*
10. Dōnum Deō dederant. *They had given a gift to God.*

F. Answer the following questions.

1. What is genitive singular case ending for the Second Declension neuter? *The ending is -ī.*
2. What is the genitive plural case ending for the First Declension? *The ending is -ārum.*
3. What is the genitive plural case ending for the Second Declension? *The ending is -ōrum.*
4. How many declensions are there? *There are five.*
5. How many conjugations are there? *There are four.*
6. Which part is the infinitive of the verb? *The Second Principal Part is the infinitive.*
7. Which case ending indicates possession? *Genitive.*
8. What is dative singular case ending for the Second Declension neuter? *The ending is -ō.*
9. What are the case endings for the Second Declension? *The case endings are us, ī, ō, um, ō, ī, ōrum, īs, ōs, īs.*
10. What the are present tense ending for the First Conjugation? *The endings are ō, s, t, mus, tis, nt.*

11. How many principal parts does a Latin verb have? *Four.*
12. Which part gives the perfect stem of the verb? *The Third Principal Part.*
13. Which case ending indicates the indirect object? *Dative.*
14. Which word in this sentence should go in the dative case? *The farmer's son gives the woman's son the gift. The word that should go in the dative is the second "son."*
15. What is a predicate nominative? *The predicate nominative is when a noun in the predicate is in the nominative case because the verb is sum.*

EXERCISE TWELVE

A. Spell out in English how each Latin word should be pronounced and place the accent properly.

1. bonus	BO nus
2. novārum	no WAH rum
3. malīs	MA lees
4. magnus	MAG nus
5. fīda	FEE da
6. parvōs	PAR wohs
7. fīdī	FEE dee
8. bonōrum	bon OH rum
9. magnum	MAG num
10. mala	MA la

B. Chant each of the following paradigms ten times through.

ō, s, t! mus, tis, nt!
bam, bās, bat! bāmus, bātis, bant!
bō, bis, bit! bimus, bitis, bunt!
a, ae, ae, am, ā! ae, ārum, īs, ās, īs!
us, ī, ō, um, ō! ī, ōrum, īs, ōs, īs!
um, ī, ō, um, ō! a, ōrum, īs, a, īs!
sum, es, est! sumus, estis, sunt!
eram, erās, erat! erāmus, erātis, erant!
erō, eris, erit! erimus, eritis, erunt!
ī, istī, it! imus, istis, ērunt!
eram, erās, erat! erāmus, erātis, erant!
erō, eris, erit! erimus, eritis, erint!

C. Translate the following review sentences.

1. Deus Fīlium dat. *God gives the Son.*
2. Poētae estis. *You are poets.*
3. Vīnum est. *It is wine.*
4. Agricola et fēmina viam spectāverant. *The farmer and woman had looked at the road.*
5. Puellae et fēminae Deum rogābunt. *The girls and women will ask God.*

6. Incolae viam dēmonstrābunt. *The inhabitants will point out (show) the road (way).*
7. Amāte! *Love!*
8. Cōnsilium dedērunt. *They gave (have given) advice.*
9. Dōnum dābunt. *They will give a gift.*
10. Deum amātis. *You love God.*

D. Translate the following English into Latin.
  1. The good son praises God. *Fīlius bonus Deum laudat.*
  2. God loved the faithful sons. *Deus filiōs fidōs amāvit.*
  3. The dear woman's little son was praising God. *Parvus fīlius carae fēminae Deum laudābat.*
  4. God loves the evil woman's happy son. *Deus fīlium laetum fēminae malae amat.*
  5. The quiet son of the trembling woman gives the faithful farmer a beautiful gift. *Fīlius quiētus fēminae trepidae dōnum pulchrum agricolae fīdō dat.*
  6. The grateful maidservant's son gives the fierce farmers a little gift. *Fīlius famulae grātae dōnum parvum agricolīs ferīs dat.*
  7. The woman's son gives the intelligent son of the farmer a great sword. *Fīlius fēminae gladium magnum fīliō acūtō agricolae dat.*
  8. The severe farmer's evil son gives the woman's just son a sword. *Fīlius malus agricolae sevērī gladium fīliō iūstō fēminae dat.*
  9. The woman's steadfast slaves give the handsome son the first sword. *Servī firmī fēminae gladium prīmum pulchrō fīliō dant.*
  10. The good slaves of the good women were giving the good girl a good gift. *Servī bonī fēminae bonae dōnum bonum puellae bonae dābant.*

E. Translate the following Latin into English.
  1. Agricolae bonī gladium fīliō dant. *The good farmers give the sword to the son.*
  2. Fēminae bonae dōnum puellīs dant. *The good women give a gift to the girls.*
  3. Fēmina et puella agricolīs dōnum bonum dant. *The woman and girl give a good gift to the farmers.*
  4. Dōnum fīliō fēminae parvae dant. *The little women give the gift to the son.*
  5. Gladium magnum fīlius fēminae dabat. *The son of the woman was giving the great sword.*
  6. Servus puellae dōnum magnum dedit. *The slave of the girl gave (has given) a great gift.*
  7. Servus fīdus agricolae gladium fīliō agricolae dabit. *The faithful slave of the farmer will give the sword to the son of the farmer.*
  8. Dōnum agricolae bonō dabis. *You will give the gift to the good farmer.*
  9. Gladium novum fīliō dabitis. *You will give the new sword to the son.*
  10. Dōnum parvum Deō dederant. *They had given the little gift to God.*

F. List all the English words you can think of which come from this lesson's vocabulary words.
  1. acute
  2. arduous
  3. bonus
  4. clarity
  5. dense
  6. firm
  7. malignant
  8. primary
  9. public
  10. pulchritude

G. Answer the following questions.

    1. What question must be answered to determine gender? *Is it masculine, feminine, or neuter?*

    2. What question must be answered to determine number? *Is it singular or plural?*

    3. What question must be answered to determine case? *Is it nominative, genitive, dative, accusative, or ablative?*

    4. What is apposition? *Apposition is when a noun is placed alongside another noun to describe it in greater detail.*

    5. What is the verb of being? *It is "sum."*

    6. Conjugate the verb of being in the imperfect tense. *It is eram, erās, erat, erāmus, erātis, erant.*

    7. Conjugate the verb of being in the future tense. *It is erō, eris, erit, erimus, eritis, erunt.*

    8. How must an adjective match the noun it modifies? *It must match in gender, number, and case.*

    9. Give an example of how an adjective may not match the noun it modifies in *appearance*. *Agricola bonus.*

    10. What is the dative, feminine plural form of the adjective *parvus*? *It is "parvārum."*

EXERCISE THIRTEEN

A. Spell out in English how each Latin word should be pronounced and place the accent properly.

1. ambulātus	am bu LAH tus
2. nāvigāvī	nah wi GAH wee
3. vulnerō	WUL ner oh
4. vulnerās	WUL ner ahs
5. gaudium	GOW di um
6. īnsulam	EEN su lam
7. amīcōs	a MEE kohs
8. hōrae	HOH reye
9. liberātus	li ber AH tus
10. oppidum	OP pi dum

B. Chant each of the following paradigms ten times through.

ō, s, t! mus, tis, nt!

bam, bās, bat! bāmus, bātis, bant!

bō, bis, bit! bimus, bitis, bunt!

a, ae, ae, am, ā! ae, ārum, īs, ās, īs!

us, ī, ō, um, ō! ī, ōrum, īs, ōs, īs!

um, ī, ō, um, ō! a, ōrum, īs, a, īs!

sum, es, est! sumus, estis, sunt!

eram, erās, erat! erāmus, erātis, erant!

erō, eris, erit! erimus, eritis, erunt!

ī, istī, it! imus, istis, ērunt!

eram, erās, erat! erāmus, erātis, erant!

erō, eris, erit! erimus, eritis, erint!

C. Translate the following review sentences.

1. Servī fēminārum puellās spectant. *The slaves of the women look at (watch) the girls.*
2. Fīlius agricolae dōnum dat. *The son of the farmer gives a gift.* or *The son of the farmer gives a gift.*
3. Fīlium fēminae spectō. *I look at (watch) the son of the woman.*
4. Servus agricolae fīlium agricolae spectāvit. *The slave of the farmer watched the farmer's son.*
5. Servum agricolae laudāverās. *You praised the farmer's slave.*
6. Servus puellae dōnum magnum dedit. *The slave gave the girl a great gift.*
7. Servus fīdus agricolae gladium fīliō agricolae dabit. *The faithful slave of the farmer will give a sword to the son of the farmer.*
8. Dōnum agricolae bonō dabis. *You will give a gift to the good farmer.*
9. Gladium novum fīliō dabitis. *You will give the new sword to the son.*
10. Dōnum parvum Deō dederant. *They had given the small gift to God.*

D. Translate the following English into Latin.

1. The good son praises God with joy. *Fīlius bonus Deum cum gaudiō laudat.*
2. The faithful son walked with the girl. *Fīlius fīdus cum puellā ambulāvit.*
3. The woman's son was wounding the farmer with a sword. *Fīlius fēminae agricolam gladiō vulnerābat.*
4. The evil woman's son walks from town. *Fīlius fēminae malae ab oppidō ambulat.*
5. God freed the son of the good woman from worry. *Deus fīlium fēminae bonae cūrā līberāverat.*
6. The woman's son gives a little gift to the messenger. *Fīlius fēminae dōnum parvum nūntiō dat.* [Teacher's Note: In this sentence *nūntiō* is in the dative case because it is the indirect object of *dat.* The English sentence would also correctly read "The woman's son gives the messenger a little gift."]
7. The woman's son walks in the town. *Fīlius fēminae in oppidō ambulat.*
8. The farmer's evil son gives the man a sword at the third hour. *Fīlius malus agricolae virō gladium tertiā hōrā dat.*
9. The woman's faithful slaves carry the sword to the son within the hour. *Servī fīdī fēminae gladium fīliō hōrā portat.*
10. The good slaves of the good women were often walking on the hidden island. *Servī bonī fēminārum bonārum saepe in īnsulā obscūrā ambulābant.*

E. Translate the following Latin into English.

1. Agricolae bonī gladium puerō dant hōra. *The good farmers give a sword to the boy within the hour.*
2. Fēminae bonae ambulābant in īnsulā. *The good women were walking on the island.*
3. Fēmina et puella ambulāvērunt ab oppidō. *The woman and girl walked from town.*
4. Amīcitiam fīliō nūntiī fēminae parvae dant. *The little women give friendship to the son of the messenger.* or *The messengers give friendship to the son of the little woman.*

5. Gladium magnum fīlius fēminae cum gaudiō dabat. *The son of the woman was giving a great sword with joy.*

6. Servus puellae agricolam gladiō magnō vulnerāvit. *The slave of the girl has wounded the farmer with a great sword.*

7. Servus fīdus agricolae gladium fīliō agricolae hōrā dabit. *The faithful slave of the farmer will give a sword to the son of the farmer within the hour.*

8. Deus agricolam līberat cūrā. *God frees the farmer from worry.*

9. Cum amīcīs navigābāmus. *We were sailing with friends.*

10. Servus agricolam gladiō vulnerat. *The slave wounds the farmer by means of a sword.*

F. Answer the following questions.

1. What is the ablative of manner? *The ablative is used to describe the way something is done.*

2. What is the ablative of time within which? *The ablative is used to describe the time within which something is done.*

3. What is the case which shows possession? *The genitive case is used to show possession.*

4. What is the ablative of separation? *The ablative is used with the noun from which something else is separated.*

5. What is the ablative of place where? *The ablative is used to describe a place where something occurs.*

6. What is the ablative of time when? *The ablative is used to describe when something occurs.*

7. What is the ablative of means? *The ablative is used to describe how something is accomplished.*

8. What is the ablative of accompaniment? *The ablative is used to describe someone who accompanies someone else.*

9. What is the ablative of place from which? *The ablative is used to describe the place which someone left.*

10. What is the fourth principal part of the verb *ambulō*? *It is* ambulātum.

EXERCISE FOURTEEN

A. Spell out in English how each Latin word should be pronounced and place the accent properly.

1. prō   proh
2. ab   ab
3. dē   day
4. ex   ex
5. sub   sub
6. in   in
7. cum   cum
8. apud   A pud
9. inter   IN ter
10. propter   PROP ter

B. Chant each of the following paradigms ten times through.

ō, s, t! mus, tis, nt!

bam, bās, bat! bāmus, bātis, bant!

bō, bis, bit! bimus, bitis, bunt!

a, ae, ae, am, ā! ae, ārum, īs, ās, īs!

us, ī, ō, um, ō! ī, ōrum, īs, ōs, īs!

um, ī, ō, um, ō! a, ōrum, īs, a, īs!

sum, es, est! sumus, estis, sunt!

eram, erās, erat! erāmus, erātis, erant!

erō, eris, erit! erimus, eritis, erunt!

ī, istī, it! imus, istis, ērunt!

eram, erās, erat! erāmus, erātis, erant!

erō, eris, erit! erimus, eritis, erint!

C. Translate the following review sentences.

1. Fīlium laudat. *He praises the Son.*
2. Nautae estis. *You are sailors.*
3. Vīnum bonum dant. *They give good wine.*
4. Agricola bonus et fēmina bona viam spectāverant. *The good farmer and good woman had looked at the road.*
5. Puellae parvae Deum amābunt. *The little girls will love God.*
6. Spectant et laudant. *They look and praise.*
7. Ambulāte! *Walk!*
8. Cōnsilium bonum dedit. *He gave good advice.*
9. Dōnum bonum dabat. *He was giving a good gift.*
10. Deum magnum laudās. *You praise a great God.*

D. Translate the following English into Latin.

1. She walks among the women. *Inter fēminās ambulat.*
2. The faithful man walked toward the road. *Vir fīdus ad viam ambulāvit.*
3. The woman's son was walking on account of the messenger. *Fīlius fēminae propter nūntium ambulābat.*
4. The evil woman's son will walk across the field. *Fīlius fēminae malae trāns agrum ambulābit.*
5. God freed the son of the good woman from worry. *Deus fīlium fēminae bonae a cūra līberāvit.*
6. The master told the boy a long story about the wind. *Dominus puerō longam fabulam dē ventō narrāvit.*
7. The woman's son will walk in front of the sailors. *Fīlius fēminae prō nautīs ambulābit.*
8. The farmer's evil son carries a sword near the table. *Fīlius malus agricolae gladium prope mēnsam portat.*
9. The woman's faithful slaves look at the sword at the house of the happy man. *Servī fīdī fēminae gladium apud virum laetum spectantt.*
10. The tired slaves of the good women were walking through the distant town. *Servī dēfessī fēminarum bonārum per oppidum longinquum ambulābant.*

E. Translate the following Latin into English.

1. Agricolae bonī ambulant ad viam. *The good farmers walk toward the road.*
2. Fēminae bonae ambulāvērunt in īnsulā. *The good women walked on the island.*
3. Fēmina et puella ambulāverint ab oppidō. *The woman and girl will have walked from town.*
4. Fēminae parvae inter puellās ambulant. *The little women walk among the girls.*
5. Gladium magnum fīlius fēminae ab oppidō portābat. *The son of the woman was carrying the great sword from town.*
6. Servus puellae circā agricolam ambulāverit. *The slave of the girl will have walked around the farmer.*
7. Servus fīdus gladium post mūrum portat. *The faithful slave carries the sword behind the wall.*
8. Ambulāvimus in oppidum. *We walked into town.*
9. Navigābāmus ad īnsulam. *We were sailing to the island.*
10. Servī agricolam trāns agrōs portant. *The slaves carry the farmer across the field.*

F. List all the English words you can think of which come from this lesson's vocabulary words.

1. approach (prope)
2. propitiate (prope)
3. proximity (prope)
4. in
5. submarine
6. anteroom
7. contary
8. intermural
9. transportation
10. post meridiem (p.m.)

G. Answer the following questions.

1. What case does *trāns* take? *It takes the accusative.*
2. How many declensions are there? *There are five declensions.*
3. What is genitive singular ending for the Second Declension? *The ending is -ī.*
4. What case does *prope* take? *It takes the accusative.*
5. What case does *contrā* take? *It takes the accusative.*
6. What does *in* mean with the ablative case? *It means "in" or "on."*
7. What case does *ab* take? *It takes the ablative.*
8. What case does *prō* take? *It takes the ablative.*
9. What does *sub* mean with the ablative case? *It means "at the foot of."*
10. What case does *dē* take? *It takes the ablative.*

EXERCISE FIFTEEN

A. Spell out in English how each Latin word should be pronounced and place the accent properly.

1. prohibeō — pro HI be oh
2. videō — WI de oh
3. videt — WI det
4. vidētis — wi DAY tis

5. habet	HA bet
6. habēmus	ha BAY mus
7. habēbit	ha BAY bit
8. prohibēbāmus	pro hi bay BAH mus
9. vidēbunt	wi DAY bunt
10. vidēbant	wi DAY bant

B. Chant each of the following paradigms ten times through.

ō, s, t! mus, tis, nt!
bam, bās, bat! bāmus, bātis, bant!
bō, bis, bit! bimus, bitis, bunt!
a, ae, ae, am, ā! ae, ārum, īs, ās, īs!
us, ī, ō, um, ō! ī, ōrum, īs, ōs, īs!
um, ī, ō, um, ō! a, ōrum, īs, a, īs!
sum, es, est! sumus, estis, sunt!
eram, erās, erat! erāmus, erātis, erant!
erō, eris, erit! erimus, eritis, erunt!
ī, istī, it! imus, istis, ērunt!
eram, erās, erat! erāmus, erātis, erant!
erō, eris, erit! erimus, eritis, erint!

C. Write the four principal parts of the following verbs. Then chant each verb "set" ten times through.

vocō, *vocō, vocāre, vocāvī, vocātum*
stō, *stō, stāre, stetī, statum*
habeō, *habeō, habēre, habuī, habitum*
moneō, *moneō, monēre, monuī, monitum*
videō, *videō, vidēre, vīdī, vīsum*

D. Translate the following review sentences.
1. Fīliōs laudat. *He praises the sons.*
2. Nautae estis. *You are sailors.*
3. Vīnum malum dant. *They give bad wine.*
4. Agricola bonus et fēmina bona gladium spectāverant. *The good farmer and good woman had looked at the sword.*
5. Puellae parvae Deum amābunt et laudābunt. *The little girls will love and praise God.*
6. Spectat et laudat. *He looks and praises.*
7. Ambulā! *Walk!*
8. Cōnsilium malum dedit. *He gave bad advice.*
9. Dōnum parvum dabat. *He was giving a little gift.*
10. Deum magnum laudātis. *You praise a great God.*

E. Translate the following English into Latin.

1. He frightens the women. *Fēminās terret.*
2. Does the faithful son see the road? *Videtne fīlius fīdus viam?*
3. The woman's son was warning the messenger. *Fīlius fēminae nūntium monēbat.*
4. The terrified woman's son will see the hidden road. *Fīlius fēminae trepidae viam obscūram vidēbit.*
5. God warns the son of the good woman. *Deus fīlium fēminae bonae monet.*
6. The woman's son has a little gift. *Fīlius fēminae dōnum parvum habet.*
7. The woman's son was warning the sailors. *Fīlius fēminae nautās monēbat.*
8. The farmer's evil son has a sword near the table, hasn't he? *Nōnne fīlius malus agricolae gladium prope mēnsam habet.*
9. The woman's faithful slaves see the sword at the house of the man. *Servī fīdī fēminae gladium apud virum vident.* (Teacher's Note: Remember that the preposition *apud* includes *of* as part of its conceptual meaning. *Apud* means *at the house of* and so the accusative case is used after *apud* rather than the genitive of possession.)
10. The bad slaves of the good women were walking. *Servī malī fēminārum bonārum ambulābant.*

F. Translate the following Latin into English.

1. Vidēmus viam. *We see the road.*
2. Nautās prohibēmus. *We keep back the sailors.*
3. Gladius fēminam terret. *The sword frightens the woman.*
4. Silvae tenebrās habent. *Forests have shadows.*
5. Gladium magnum fīlius fēminae vidēbat. *The son of the woman was seeing the great sword.*
6. Servum puellae vidēbitis. *You (pl.) will see the slave of the girl.*
7. Servus fīdus gladium vidēbat. *The faithful slave was seeing the sword.*
8. Perīculī oppidum impendent. *Dangers hang over the town.*
9. Copiae fēminam prohibent. *The troops keep back the woman.*
10. Agricolae carrōs complēbunt. *The farmers will fill the carts.*

G. List all the English words you can think of which come from this lesson's vocabulary words.

1. television
2. video
3. admonish
4. prohibit
5. evident

6. providential
7. view
8. premonition
9. monitor
10. habit

H. Answer the following questions.

1. What case does *sub* take? *It takes either ablative or accusative, depending upon what you want it to mean.*
2. How many conjugations are there? *There are four.*
3. What is genitive plural ending for the Second Declension? *The ending is -ōrum.*
4. What case does *post* take? *It takes the accusative.*
5. What case does *in* take? *It takes either ablative or accusative, depending upon what you want it*

to mean.

6. How is the stem for the Second Conjugation found? *It is found by dropping the* -re *from the Second Principal Part.*
7. Are the endings for the imperfect tense the same for the First and Second Conjugations? *Yes, they are.*
8. What the endings for the future tense in the Second Conjugation? *bō, bis, bit, bimus, bitus, bunt.*
9. How would one command more than one person *to see*? *Vidēte!*
10. What is the second person, plural ending, imperfect tense for the verb *video*? *Vidēbatis.*

READING ONE

PECUNIA OBSCURA

Puerī et puellae prope harēnam ambulābant. Parvam īnsulam vidēbant. Nautae famās dē pecūniā latebrā in īnsulā narrāvērunt. Līberī laetī semper amābant explorāre. Altē cōgitāvērunt. Mox carrum appropinquāvērunt et laborāvērunt. Rotās ā carrō removērunt. Tum carrum sine rotīs in aquam locāvērunt. Ad īnsulam navigāvērunt. Terram cum diligentiā spectāvērunt. Dēmōnstrābitne īnsula līberīs latebram argentī?

TRANSLATION:
The boys and girls were walking near the beach. They saw (were seeing) a small island. The sailors have told stories about hidden money on the island. The happy children always liked to explore. (Imperfect tense because they were habitual explorers, they did it frequently over an undetermined period of time.) They thought hard. (Perfect tense because they finished it.) Soon they approached a cart and they worked. They removed the wheels from the cart. Then they placed the cart without wheels into the water. They sailed to the island. They looked at the ground with diligence. Will the island show (to) the children the hiding place of the money?

QUESTIONS:
Comprehension:
A correct answer is given. Other correctly composed answers may be accepted.
1. Ubi līberī ambulābant? *Līberī prope harēnam ambulābant.*
2. Cūr rotās ā carrō removērunt? *Rotās removērunt trāns aquam navigāre.*
3. Ubi puerī et puellae navigāvērunt? *Ad īnsulam navigāvērunt.*

Grammar:
Give the case and the reason for the use of that case for the following words:
1. (line 1) pecūniā   *Ablative case, used as object of the preposition, "dē."*
2. (line 2) laetī   *Nominative case, adjective modifying "līberī."*
3. (line 2) carrum   *Accusative case, direct object of the sentence.*
4. (line 3) rotīs   *Ablative case, used as object of the preposition "sine."*
5. (line 5) diligentiā   *Ablative case, ablative of manner (cum + noun).*

EXERCISE SIXTEEN

A. Spell out in English how each Latin word should be pronounced and place the accent properly.

1. monuī	MON u ee
2. vīdī	WEE dee
3. habuī	HA bu ee
4. prohibuī	pro HI bu ee
5. monuistī	mo nu IS tee
6. habuistis	ha bu IS tis
7. vīdistis	wee DIS tis
8. prohibuērunt	pro hi bu AY runt
9. vīderam	WEE de ram
10. vīderō	WEE de roh

B. Chant each of the following paradigms ten times through.

ō, s, t! mus, tis, nt!
bam, bās, bat! bāmus, bātis, bant!
bō, bis, bit! bimus, bitis, bunt!
a, ae, ae, am, ā! ae, ārum, īs, ās, īs!
us, ī, ō, um, ō! ī, ōrum, īs, ōs, īs!
um, ī, ō, um, ō! a, ōrum, īs, a, īs!
sum, es, est! sumus, estis, sunt!
eram, erās, erat! erāmus, erātis, erant!
erō, eris, erit! erimus, eritis, erunt!
ī, istī, it! imus, istis, ērunt!
eram, erās, erat! erāmus, erātis, erant!
erō, eris, erit! erimus, eritis, erint!

C. Write the four principal parts of the following verbs. Then chant each verb "set" ten times through.

amō, *amō, amāre, amāvī, amātum*
clamō, *clamō, clamāre, clamāvī, clamātum*
caleō, *caleō, calēre, caluī, calitum*
compleō, *compleō, complēre, complevī, complētum*
iaceō, *iaceō, iacēre, iacuī,* - - - - *(no fourth principal part)*

D. Decline:

mensa, *mensae, mensae, mensam, mensā, mensae, mensārum, mensīs, mensās, mensīs*
servus, *servī, servō, servum, servō, servī, servōrum, servīs, servōs, servīs*
antrum, *antrī, antrō, antrum, antrō, antra, antrōrum, antrīs, antra, antrīs*

E. Conjugate:

voco, *vocās, vocat, vocāmus, vocātis, vocant;*
vocābam, vocābās, vocābat, vocābāmus, vocābātis, vocābant;
vocābō, vocābis, vocābit, vocābimus, vocābitis, vocābunt;
vocāvī, vocāvistī, vocāvit, vocāvimus, vocāvistis, vocāvērunt;
vocāveram, vocāverās, vocāverat, vocāverāmus, vocāverātis, vocāverant;
vocāverō, vocāveris, vocāverit, vocāverimus, vocāveritis, vocāverint.

video, *vidēs, videt, vidēmus, vidētis, vident;*
vidēbam, vidēbās, vidēbat, vidēbāmus, vidēbātis, vidēbant;
vidēbō, vidēbis, vidēbit, vidēbimus, vidēbitis, vidēbunt;
vīdī, vīdistī, vīdit, vīdimus, vīdistis, vīdērunt;
vīderam, vīderās, vīderat, vīderāmus, vīderātis, vīderant;
vīderō, vīderis, vīderit, vīderimus, vīderitis, vīderint.

F. Translate the following review sentences.

1. Fīliōs videō. *I see the sons.*
2. Nautās vidēs. *You see the sailors.*
3. Fēmina et puella ambulāverint ab oppidō. *The woman and girl will have walked from town.*
4. Fēminae parvae inter puellās ambulant. *The little women walk among the girls.*
5. Gladium magnum fīlius fēminae ab oppidō portābat. *The son of the woman was carrying the great sword from town.*
6. Servus puellae circā agricolam ambulāverit. *The slave of the girl will have walked around the farmer.*
7. Servus fīdus gladium post mūrum portat. *The faithful slave carries the sword behind the wall.*
8. Cōnsilium malum dabit. *He will give bad advice.*
9. Dōnum parvum dabunt. *They will give a little gift.*
10. Deum magnum laudās. *You praise a great God.*

G. Translate the following English into Latin.

1. She saw the women with a man. *Fēminās cum virō vīdit.*
2. The faithful son had seen the road. *Fīlius fīdus viam vīderat.*
3. The woman's son warned the messenger about the danger. *Fīlius fēminae nūntium dē perīculō monuit.*
4. The evil woman's son will have seen the road within the hour. *Fīlius fēminae malae viam horā vīderit.*
5. God warned the son of the good woman. *Deus fīlium fēminae bonae monuit.*
6. The woman's son had a little gift. *Fīlius fēminae dōnum parvum habuit.*
7. The woman's son saw the sailors near the cave. *Fīlius fēminae nautās prope antrum vīdit.*
8. The farmer's evil son will have had a sword on the table. *Fīlius malus agricolae gladium in mēnsā habuerit.*
9. The woman's faithful slaves had seen the sword at the house of the son. *Servī fīdī fēminae gladium apud fīlium vīderant.*
10. The bad slaves of the good women walked. *Servī malī fēminae bonae ambulāvērunt.*

H. Translate the following Latin into English.

1. Vīdimus viam ad antrum. *We saw the road to the cave.*
2. Nautās prohibuī. *I kept back the sailors.*
3. Laeta fēmina gladium habuit. *The happy woman had the sword.*
4. Fēminae bonum vīnum habuērunt. *The women had good wine.*
5. Fīlius fēminae gladium magnum vīdit. *The son of the woman saw the great sword.*
6. Servus puellae propter flammam caluerit. *The slave of the girl will have been warm because of the flame.*
7. Gladius servum fīdum placuit. *The sword pleased the faithful servant.*
8. Vīdistisne ē fenestrā oppidum? *Did you see (have you seen) the town from the window?*
9. Servus fēminam prohibuerat. *The slave had kept back the woman.*
10. Servī agricolam monuērunt. *The slaves have warned the farmer.*

I. Answer the following questions.

1. What is the accusative plural form of *dōnum*? *It is* dōna.
2. What is the genitive singular ending for the Second Declension? *The ending is* -ī.
3. What is genitive singular ending for the First Declension? *The ending is* -ae.
4. What case does *circā* take? *It takes the accusative.*
5. What does *in* mean when it is followed by the accusative? *It means* into.
6. What is the third principal part for the verb *videō*? *The Third Principal Part is* "vīdī."
7. Are the endings for the pluperfect tense the same for the First and Second Conjugations? *They are the same.*
8. What are the endings for the future perfect tense in the Second Conjugation? *They are* erō, eris, erit, erimus, eritis, erint.
9. How would one command more than one person *to warn*? *Monēte!*
10. What is the second person, plural ending, future perfect tense for the verb *videō*? *Vīderitis.*

Exercise Seventeen

A. Spell out in English how each Latin word should be pronounced and place the accent properly.

1. monuit	MO nu it
2. vīdimus	WEE di mus
3. habuērunt	ha bu AY runt
4. prohibuistī	pro hi bu IS tee
5. monuī	MO nu ee
6. habuistī	ha bu IS tee
7. vīdī	WEE dee
8. prohibuī	pro HI bu ee
9. vīderās	WEE de rahs
10. vīderit	WEE de rit

B. Chant each of the following paradigms ten times through.

ō, s, t! mus, tis, nt!

bam, bās, bat! bāmus, bātis, bant!

bō, bis, bit! bimus, bitis, bunt!

a, ae, ae, am, ā! ae, ārum, īs, ās, īs!

us, ī, ō, um, ō! ī, ōrum, īs, ōs, īs!

um, ī, ō, um, ō! a, ōrum, īs, a, īs!

sum, es, est! sumus, estis, sunt!

eram, erās, erat! erāmus, erātis, erant!

erō, eris, erit! erimus, eritis, erunt!

ī, istī, it! imus, istis, ērunt!

eram, erās, erat! erāmus, erātis, erant!

erō, eris, erit! erimus, eritis, erint!

C. Write the four principal parts of the following verbs. Then chant each verb "set" ten times through.

conciliō, *conciliō, conciliāre, conciliāvī, conciliātum*

conservō, *conservō, conservāre, conservāvī, conservātum*

dō, *dō, dare, dedī, datum*

impendeō, *impendeō, impendēre, impendī, impensum*

placeō, *placeō, placēre, placuī, placitum*

D. Decline:

cūra, *cura, curae, curae, curam, curā, curae, curārum, curīs, curās, curīs*

vir, *vir, virī, virō, virum, virō, virī, virōrum, virīs, virōs, virīs*

novum vallum, *novum vallum, novī vallī, novō vallō, novum vallum, nova valla, novōrum vallōrum, novīs vallīs, nova valla, novīs vallīs*

Challenge:

bonus agricola, *bonus agricola, bonī agricolae, bonō agricolae, bonum agricolam, bonō agricolā, bonī agricolae, bonōrum agricolārum, bonīs agricolīs, bonōs agricolās, bonīs agricolīs*

E. Translate the following review sentences.

1. Fīliōs vīdī. *I saw the sons.*

2. Nautās vīdistī. *You saw the sailors.*

3. Vīnum habuī. *I had wine.*

4. Agricola malus et fēmina parva gladium vidēbunt. *The bad farmer and little woman will see the sword.*

5. Puellae parvae Deum amāvērunt. *The little girls loved God.*

6. Spectāvimus et laudāvimus. *We looked and praised.*

7. Amāte! *Love!*

8. Cōnsilium malum dedit. *He gave bad advice.*

9. Dōnum parvum dabant. *They were giving a little gift.*

10. Deum magnum laudātis. *You praise a great God.*

F. Translate the following English into Latin.

  1. She saw the women with many dishes. *Fēminās cum multīs patellīs vīdit.*

  2. Soon the faithful son had seen the long road. *Mox filius fidus viam longam vīderat.*

  3. Then the woman's son will have warned the messenger. *Tum filius fēminae nūntium monuerit.*

  4. The evil woman's son saw the great sword in the dark cave. *Fīlius fēminae malae gladium magnum in obscūrō (or nigrō) antrō vīdit.*

  5. God will warn the good son of the faithful woman. *Deus filium bonum fēminae fidae monēbit.*

  6. The woman's son carried wine to the table. *Filius fēminae vīnum ad mensam portāvit.*

  7. The messenger will have seen the sailors with the money. *Nuntius nautās cum pecūniā vīderit.*

  8. The farmer's good son had a great sword near the door. *Filius bonus agricolae gladium magnum prope portam habuit.*

  9. The woman's faithful slaves had seen the sword of the son. *Servī fidī fēminae gladium filiī vīderant.*

  10. The good slaves of the bad women always walked with great care in the town. *Servī bonī fēminārum malārum semper magnā (cum) diligentiā ambulāvērunt.*

G. Translate the following Latin into English.

  1. Vīdī viam. *I saw the road.*

  2. Nautās prohibuit. *He kept back the sailors.*

  3. Fēminae gladium habuērunt. *The women had a sword.*

  4. Fēminae vīnum habuerint. *The women will have had wine.*

  5. Gladium magnum filius fēminae vīderit. *The son of the woman will have seen the great sword.*

  6. Servus puellae vīderat. *The slave of the girl had seen.*

  7. Servus fidus gladium videt. *The faithful slave sees the sword.*

  8. Vīdistis oppida. *You saw the towns.*

  9. Servus fēminās prohibuerit. *The slave will have kept back the women.*

  10. Servī agricolās vīderint. *The slaves will have seen the farmers.*

H. Give a synopsis of the following verbs.

  1. videō—third person, singular

    videt

    vidēbat

    vidēbit

    vīdit

    vīderat

    vīderit

  2. laudō—second person, plural

    laudātis

    laudābātis

    laudābitis

    laudāvistis

    laudāverātis

    laudāveritis

   3. ambulō—first person, singular
     ambulō
     ambulābam
     ambulābō
     ambulāvī
     ambulāveram
     ambulāverō
   4. portō—third person, plural
     portant
     portābant
     portābunt
     portāvērunt
     portāverant
     portāverint
   5. dō—second person, singular
     dās (Remember that the first and second person present of *dō* are the only forms in the Active System which have the macron.)
     dabās
     dabis
     dedistī
     dederās
     dederis
   6. habeō—first person, plural
     habēmus
     habēbāmus
     habēbimus
     habuimus
     habuerāmus
     habuerimus

I. Answer the following questions.

   1. What is the accusative plural form of *oppidum*? *It is "oppida."*
   2. What is the genitive singular ending for the First Declension? *It is -ae.*
   3. What is dative plural ending for the Second Declension? *It is -īs.*
   4. What case does *apud* take? *It takes the accusative.*
   5. What does *in* mean when it is followed by the ablative? *It means "in" or "on."*
   6. What is the third principal part for the verb *dō*? *It is "dedī."*
   7. What do you do when you give a synopsis of a verb? *You give a sample from each one of the tenses of a particular person and number.*
   8. What do you do when you conjugate a verb? *You give each person and number in a particular tense.*
   9. How would one command just one person *to love*? *Amā!*
   10. What is the first person, plural ending, future perfect tense for the verb *habeō*? *Habuerimus.*

READING TWO

There is no vocabulary list for this lesson because most of the meanings can be derived from the English derivatives and the list of instruments is too specialized for a student memory lesson.

PSALMUS 150

¹Alleluia.
Laudāte Dominum in sanctīs eius;
Laudāt eum in firmamentō virtūtis eius.
² Laudāte eum in virtūtibus eius,
Laudāte eum secundum multitūdinem magnitūdinis eius.
³ Laudāte eum in sonō tubae;
Laudāte eum in psalteriō et citharāā.
⁴ Laudāte eum in tympanō et chorō;
Laudāte eum in chordīs et organō.
⁵ Laudāte eum in cymbalīs benesonantibus;
Laudāte eum in cymbalīs iubilationis.
⁶ Omnis spiritus [laudāte] Dominum! Alleluia.

TRANSLATION (FROM THE NEW INTERNATIONAL VERSION)
*¹ Praise the L*ORD*.*
Praise God in his sanctuary;
praise him in his mighty heavens.
² Praise him for his acts of power;
praise him for his surpassing greatness.
³ Praise him with the sounding of trumpet,
praise him with the harp and lyre,
⁴ praise him with tambourine and dancing,
praise him with the strings and flute,
⁵ praise him with the clash of cymbals,
praise him with resounding cymbals.
*⁶ Let everything that has breath praise the L*ORD*.*
*Praise the L*ORD*.*

QUESTIONS:
1. What form of the verb is *laudāte*? *It is the imperative form of the verb* laudō.
2. In this passage, what is the best translation of *in* (verses 3-5)? *Probably the best translation is* "on", *or* "upon".
3. What case is used for all the instruments in verses 4 and 5? Why is this case used? *The ablative case is used. It could be considered ablative of place where (on the instruments) or as a later Vulgate leaves out the prepositions, it could be ablative of means (by means of the specific instruments).*

CHALLENGE:
Look up this psalm in several translations of the Bible. How are the translations different? Which translation most closely matches this Latin version? *The answer to these questions will be determined by which versions are chosen for comparison.*

EXERCISE EIGHTEEN

A. Spell out in English how each Latin word should be pronounced and place the accent properly.

1. mātris		MAH tris
2. lūcibus		LOO ki bus
3. patrem		PA trem
4. mātrēs		MAH trays
5. rēgibus		RAY gil bus
6. lēgibus		LAY gi bus
7. lēge		LAY ge
8. patribus		PA tri bus
9. mātrum		MAH trum
10. montibus		MON ti bus

B. Chant each of the following paradigms ten times through.

is, is, ī, em, e! ēs, um, ibus, ēs, ibus!

ī, istī, it! imus, istis, ērunt!

eram, erās, erat! erāmus, erātis, erant!

erō, eris, erit! erimus, eritis, erint!

C. Chant each of the following paradigms two times through.

ō, s, t! mus, tis, nt!

bam, bās, bat! bāmus, bātis, bant!

bō, bis, bit! bimus, bitis, bunt!

a, ae, ae, am, ! ae, rum, īs, s, īs!

us, ī, ō, um, ō! ī, ōrum, īs, ōs, īs!

um, ī, ō, um, ō! a, ōrum, īs, a, īs!

sum, es, est! sumus, estis, sunt!

eram, ers, erat! erāmus, erātis, erant!

erō, eris, erit! erimus, eritis, erunt!

D. Write the four principal parts of the following verbs. Then chant each verb "set" ten times through.

convocō, *convocō, convocāre, convocāvī, convocātum*

errō, *errō, errāre, errāvī, errātum*

explorō, *explorō, explorāre, explorāvī, explorātum*

prohibeō, *prohibeō, prohibēre, prohibuī, prohibitum*
terreō, *terreō, terrēre, terruī, territum*

E. Decline:

peritus discipulus, *perītī discipulī, perītō discipulō, perītum discipulum, perītō discipulō, perītī discipulī, perītōrum discipulōrum, perītīs discipulīs, perītōs discipulōs, perītīs discipulīs*

prīmum exemplum, *primī exemplī, primō exemplō, primum exemplum, primō exemplō, prima exempla, primōrum exemplōrum, primīs exemplīs, prima exempla, primīs exemplīs*

Challenge:

parva avis, *parvae avis, parvae avī, parvam avem, parvā ave, parvae avēs, parvārum avium, parvīs avibus, parvās avēs, parvīs avibus*

F. Translate the following review sentences.

1. Fīliōs vīdistī. *You saw (have seen) the sons.*
2. Nautās vīdī. *I saw the sailors.*
3. Bonum vīnum habuī. *I had good wine.*
4. Agricola et fēmina parva gladiōs habuērunt. *The farmer and little woman had swords.*
5. Parvae puellae fēminās amāvērunt. *The little girls loved the women.*
6. Laudāverant. *They had praised.*
7. Laudāte! *Praise!*
8. Malum cōnsilium malus agricola laudāvit. *The evil farmer praised the bad advice.*
9. Parvum dōnum laudābant. *They were praising the little gift.*
10. Magnum Deum amāmus. *We love a great God.*

G. Translate the following English into Latin.

1. She saw the king with the troops. *Rēgem cum cōpiīs vīdit.*
2. The faithful son had seen the mountains from the window of the farmhouse. *Fīlius fīdus montēs ā fenestrā villae vīderat.*
3. The king's son will have warned the scout about the swamp. *Fīlius rēgis explōrātōrem dē palūde monuerit.*
4. The evil king saw the great fire from the mountain. *Rēx malus ā monte magnum ignem vīdit.*
5. God will warn the small son of the father and mother. *Deus parvum fīlium patris et mātris monēbit.*
6. The king's grandson walked to the mountain with the old man. *Nepōs rēgis ad montem cum sene ambulāvit.*
7. The young woman will have pleased the guest with flowers. *Virgō hospem flōribus placuerit.*
8. The farmer's strength kept back the cattle. *Virtūs agricolae bovēs prohibuit .*
9. The woman's faithful slaves had pleased the mother of the girl. *Servī fīdī fēminae mātrem puellae placuerant.*
10. The bad slaves of the good father walked from the town. *Malī servī patris bonī ex oppidō ambulāvērunt.*

H. Translate the following Latin into English.

1. Vīdī lūcem. *I saw the light.*
2. Patrēs prohibuit. *He kept back the fathers.*
3. Mātrēs ignem habuērunt. *The mothers had fire.*
4. Pater vīnum laudāverat. *Father had praised the wine.*
5. Rēx fīlium fēminae vīderit. *The king will have seen the son of the woman.*
6. Servus lēgēs laudat. *The slave praises the laws.*
7. Servus rēgem videt. *The slave sees the king.*
8. Vīdistis montēs. *You saw the mountains.*
9. Servus mātrēs prohibuerit. *The slave will have kept back the mothers.*
10. Servī rēgem vīderint. *The slaves will have seen the king.*
11. Mercātor lapidem pulchrum magnī aedificiī rēgis laudāvit. *The merchant praised the beautiful stone of the great building of the king.*
12. Pastor vallum longum flōribus complēvit. *The shepherd filled the long wall with flowers.*
13. Rēx leōnēs ferōs in silvā prope turrim virgōnis habēbat. *The king was holding the fierce lions in the forest near the maiden's tower.*
14. Lūx pastōrī laetō magnam saepem inter silvam et turrim dēmōnstrāvit. *The light showed the glad shepherd a great hedge between the forest and the tower.*
15. Juvenis virginem trepidam per tempestātem horrendam appropinquāvit. *The youth approached the trembling maiden through the dreadful storm.*

I. Give a synopsis of the following verbs.

1. videō—third person, plural
   vident
   vidēbant
   vidēbunt
   vīdērunt
   vīderant
   vīderint

2. laudō—second person, singular
   laudās
   laudābās
   laudābis
   laudāvistī
   laudāverās
   laudāveris

3. ambulō—first person, plural
   ambulāmus
   ambulābāmus
   ambulābimus
   ambulāvimus
   ambulāverāmus
   ambulāverimus

4. portō—third person, singular
  portat
  portābat
  portābit
  portāvit
  portāverat
  portāverit

5. dō—second person, plural
  datis
  dabātis
  dabitis
  dedistis
  dederātis
  dederitis

6. habeō—first person, singular
  habeō
  habēbam
  habēbō
  habuī
  habueram
  habuerō

J. List all the English words you can think of which come from this lesson's vocabulary words.

  1. paternal   6. regal
  2. maternal   7. legal
  3. maternity   8. legislature
  4. Lucifer   9. ignition
  5. patristic   10. nocturnal

K. Answer the following questions.

  1. What is the ablative plural form of *gladius*? *It is "gladiīs."*
  2. How many conjugations are there? *There are four.*
  3. What is nominative plural ending for the Second Declension? *The ending is -ī.*
  4. What cases does *sub* take? *It takes either ablative or accusative, depending upon what you want it to say.*
  5. List several uses of the ablative case.
  6. What is the third principal part for the verb *ambulō*? *The Third Principal Part is "ambulāvī."*
  7. What is the ablative plural ending for the Third Declension? *The ending is -ibus.*
  8. What is the accusative singular ending for the Third Declension? *The ending is -em.*
  9. What is the accusative singular form of the word *māter*? *It is "mātrem."*
  10. What is the dative plural form of the word *mōns*? *It is "montibus."*

EXERCISE NINETEEN

A. Spell out in English how each Latin word should be pronounced and place the accent properly.

1. mātribus	MAH tri bus
2. lūx	loox
3. pater	PA ter
4. mātrem	MAH trem
5. rēgis	RAY gis
6. lēgis	LAY gis
7. lēgēs	LAY gays
8. patrēs	PA trays
9. mātribus	MAH tri bus
10. temporis	TEM po ris

B. Chant each of the following paradigms ten times through.

is, is, ī, em, e! ēs, um, ibus, ēs, ibus!
ī, istī, it! imus, istis, ērunt!
eram, erās, erat! erāmus, erātis, erant!
erō, eris, erit! erimus, eritis, erint!

C. Chant each of the following paradigms two times through.

ō, s, t! mus, tis, nt!
bam, bās, bat! bāmus, bātis, bant!
bō, bis, bit! bimus, bitis, bunt!
a, ae, ae, am, ā! ae, ārum, īs, ās, īs!
us, ī, ō, um, ō! ī, ōrum, īs, ōs, īs!
um, ī, ō, um, ō! a, ōrum, īs, a, īs!
sum, es, est! sumus, estis, sunt!
eram, erās, erat! erāmus, erātis, erant!
erō, eris, erit! erimus, eritis, erunt!

D. Write the four principal parts of the following verbs. Then chant each verb "set" ten times through.

habitō, *habitō, habitāre, habitāvī, habitātum*
laborō, *laborō, laborāre, laborāvī, laborātum*
laudō, *laudō, laudāre, laudāvī, laudātum*
videō, *videō, vidēre, vīdī, vīsum*
caleō, *caleō, calēre, caluī, calitum*

E. Decline:

> [Teacher's Note: Astute students may notice that some adjectives precede the nouns while others follow the nouns they modify. In formal Latin, as in other Romance languages, most adjectives follow the nouns. In Latin, adjectives which usually precede the noun are: *bonus, malus, magnus, multus, parvus,* and *tōtus.*]

parvum antrum, *parvī antrī, parvō antrō, parvum antrum, parvō antrō, parva antra, parvōrum antrōrum, parvīs antrīs, parva antra, parvīs antrīs*

flōs novus, *flōris novī, flōrī novō, flōrem novum, flōre novō, flōrēs novī, flōrum novōrum, flōribus novīs, flōrēs novōs, flōribus novīs*

lītus pulchrum, *lītoris pulchrī, lītorī pulchrō, lītus pulchrum, lītore pulchrō, lītora pulchra, lītorum pulchōrum, lītoribus pulchrīs, lītora pulchra, lītoribus pulchrīs*

Challenge: iter asperum (Hint: *iter* is an i-stem noun)

iter asperum, *itineris asperī, itinerī asperō, iter asperum, itinerī asperō, itineria aspera, itinerium asperōrum, itineribus asperīs, itineria aspera, itineribus asperīs*

F. Translate the following review sentences.
1. Montem vīdistī. *You saw the mountain.*
2. Montēs vīdī. *I saw the mountains.*
3. Ignem bonum habuī. *I had a good fire.*
4. Fēmina parva ignem habet. *The little woman has fire.*
5. Puellae parvae matrēs laudāvērunt. *The little girls praised the mothers.*
6. Laudāverint. *They will have praised.*
7. Portā! *Carry!*
8. Noctem agricola malus vīdit. *The evil farmer saw the night.*
9. Dōnum parvum spectābant. *They were looking at the little gift.*
10. Deum magnum amant. *They love a great God.*

G. Translate the following English into Latin.
1. The tired king saw the fire from the distant hill. *Rēx dēfessus ignem ā colle longinquō vīdit.*
2. The faithful son had seen the sheep. *Fīlius fīdus gregem vīderat.*
3. The journey will have pleased the son of the king. *Iter fīlium rēgis placuerit.*
4. The grateful people praised the just laws. *Populus grātus lēgēs iustōs laudāvit.*

> [Teacher's Note: *populus* is used to refer to a group of people. If it is used in the plural, it refers to many tribes or people groups.]

5. God will warn the son of the faithful father. *Deus fīlium patris fīdī monuerit.*
6. Time praised the king's son. *Tempus fīlium rēgis laudāvit.*
7. The woman's happy son walked into the quiet night. *Fīlius laetus fēminae in noctem quiētam ambulāvit.*
8. The king loved the laws of God. *Rēx lēgēs Deī amāvit.*
9. Do the songs of children please good mothers? *Placentne carminia līberōrum bonās mātrēs?*
10. The Law of God does not have bad laws. *Lēx Deī lēgēs malās nōn habet.*

H. Translate the following Latin into English.

  1. Ad rēgem gladium portō. *I carry the sword to the king.*
  2. Lītus flumen ab urbe prohibuit. *The shoreline kept the river from the city.*
  3. Māter ignem habet. *Mother has fire.*
  4. Pater vīnum prohibuit. *Father kept back the wine.*
  5. Rēx fīlium mātris vīderit. *The king will have seen the son of the mother.*
  6. Lēx Deī famulum laudat. *The law of God praises the slave (the manservant).*
  7. Lēx Deī bonum rēgem placuerat. *The law of God had pleased the good king.*
  8. Montem vīdistī. *You saw the mountain.*
  9. Servī animalia prohibuerant. *The slaves had kept the animals back.*
  10. Servī rēgem vidēbant. *The slaves were seeing the king.*

I. Give a synopsis of the following verbs.

  1. videō—first person, plural
     vidēmus
     vidēbāmus
     vidēbimus
     vīdimus
     vīderāmus
     vīderimus

  2. laudō—third person, singular
     laudat
     laudābat
     laudābit
     laudāvit
     laudāverat
     laudāverit

  3. ambulō—second person, plural
     ambulātis
     ambulābātis
     ambulābitis
     ambulāvistis
     ambulāverātis
     ambulāveritis

  4. portō—first person, singular
     portō
     portābam
     portābō
     portāvī
     portāveram
     portāverō

5. dō—third person, plural
   dant
   dabant
   dabunt
   dedērunt
   dederant
   dederint
6. habeō—second person, singular
   habēs
   habēbās
   habēbis
   habuistī
   habuerās
   habueris

J. List all the English words you can think of which come from this lesson's vocabulary words.

1. temporary
2. temporal
3. time
4. tense
5. temperance
6. temporize
7. extemporaneous
8. contemporary
9. temper
10. tempest

K. Answer the following questions.

1. What is the ablative plural form of *ignis*? *The form is* "ignibus."
2. How many declensions are there? *There are five.*
3. What is nominative singular ending for the Second Declension? *The ending is* -us.
4. What case does *post* take? *It takes the accusative.*
5. List two uses of the ablative case. *Ablative of means, and Ablative of manner.*
6. What is the third principal part for the verb *habeō*? *The Third Principal Part is* "habuī."
7. What is the ablative singular ending for the Third Declension Neuter? *The ending is* -e.
8. What two cases are the same in the Third Declension Neuter? *The two cases that are the same are the Nominative and Accusative.*
9. What is the accusative plural form of the word *tempus*? *The form is* "tempora."
10. What is the dative singular form of the word *mōns*? *The form is* "montī."

Exercise Twenty

A. Spell out in English how each Latin word should be pronounced and place the accent properly.

1. facilibus		fa KI li bus
2. fortī		FOR tee
3. gravis		GRA wis
4. similīs		SI mi lees
5. similem		SI mi lem
6. omnēs		OM nays
7. breve		BRE we
8. ācribus		AH kri bus
9. ācre		AH kre
10. forte		FOR te

B. Chant each of the following paradigms ten times through.

is, is, ī, em, e! ēs, um, ibus, ēs, ibus!

ī, istī, it! imus, istis, ērunt!

eram, erās, erat! erāmus, erātis, erant!

erō, eris, erit! erimus, eritis, erint!

C. Chant each of the following paradigms two times through.

ō, s, t! mus, tis, nt!

bam, bās, bat! bāmus, bātis, bant!

bō, bis, bit! bimus, bitis, bunt!

a, ae, ae, am, ā! ae, ārum, īs, ās, īs!

us, ī, ō, um, ō! ī, ōrum, īs, ōs, īs!

um, ī, ō, um, ō! a, ōrum, īs, a, īs!

sum, es, est! sumus, estis, sunt!

eram, erās, erat! erāmus, erātis, erant!

erō, eris, erit! erimus, eritis, erunt!

D. Write the four principal parts of the following verbs. Then chant each verb "set" ten times through.

mandō, *mandō, mandāre, mandāvī, mandātum*

mutō, *mutō, mutāre, mutāvī, mutātum*

narrō, *narrō, narrāre, narrāvī, narrātum*

compleō, *compleō, complēre, complēvī, complētum*

habeō, *habeō, habēre, habuī, habitum*

E. Decline:

īnsula mea, *īnsulae meae, īnsulae meae, īnsulam meam, īnsulā meā, īnsulae meae, īnsulārum meārum, īnsulīs meīs, īnsulās meās, īnsulīs meīs*

lūx clara, *lūcis clarae, lūcī clarae, lūcem claram, lūce clarā, lūcēs clarae, lūcum clarārum, lūcibus clārīs, lūcēs clarās, lūcibus clārīs*

rēx fortis, *rēgis fortis, rēgī fortī, rēgem fortem, rēge fortī, rēgēs fortēs, rēgum fortium, rēgibus fortibus, rēgēs fortēs, rēgibus fortibus*

Challenge:

gaudium breve, *gaudiī brevis, gaudiō brevī, gaudium breve, gaudiō brevī, gaudia brevia, gaudiōrum brevium, gaudiīs brevibus, gaudia brevia, gaudiīs brevibus*

F. Translate the following review sentences.

1. Puellās spectābāmus. *We were looking at the girls.*
2. Puellam laudābant. *They were praising the girl.*
3. Poēta et agricola Deum laudābant. *The poet and farmer were praising God.*
4. Agricola puellam spectat. *The farmer looks at the girl.*
5. Agricolae nōn sumus. *We are not farmers.*
6. Nauta nōn est. *He is not a sailor.*
7. Porte! *Carry!*
8. Fēminae et puellae vocāvērunt. *The women and girls called.*
9. Dōnum magnum spectābant. *They were looking at the great gift.*
10. Christus Deus est. *Christ is God.*

G. Translate the following English into Latin.

1. The brave king saw the fire. *Rēx fortis ignem vīdit.*
2. The brave son had seen the night. *Fīlius fortis noctem vīderat.*
3. The mother will have warned the strong son of the serious king. *Māter fīlium fortem rēgis gravis monuerit.*
4. The grave king praised all just laws. *Rēx gravis lēgēs omnēs iūstās laudāvit.*
5. God will warn all sons of faithful fathers. *Deus fīliōs omnēs patrum fīdōrum monēbit.*
6. The dog has frightened the swift son. *Canis fīlium celerem terruit.*
7. The woman's brave son walked into the fierce night. *Fīlius fortis fēminae in noctem ācrem ambulāvit.*
8. All kings do not love the laws of God. *Rēgēs omnēs lēgēs Deī nōn amant.*
9. The law of God does not praise fierce sailors. *Lēx Deī nautās ācrēs nōn laudat.*
10. The law of God does not praise all girls. *Lēx Deī puellās omnēs nōn laudat.*

H. Translate the following Latin into English.

1. Ad rēgem fortem gladium portō. *I carry the sword to the brave king.*
2. Tempus vocāvit. *Time called.*
3. Māter gravis ignem habet. *The serious mother has fire.*

4. Pater vīnum similem laudāvit. *Father praised the similar wine.*

5. Rēgēs omnēs fīlium mātris vīderint. *All kings will have seen the son of the mother.*

6. Lēx Deī servum brevem laudat. *The law of God praises the short slave.*

7. Lēx Deī rēgem fortem laudāverat. *The law of God had praised the brave king.*

8. Montem omnem vīdistī. *You saw each mountain.*

9. Servī fortēs mātrem prohibuerant. *The brave slaves had kept back the mother.*

10. Servī rēgem fortem vidēbant. *The slaves were seeing the brave king.*

I. Give a synopsis of the following verbs.

  1. vocō—first person, plural
> *vocāmus*
> *vocābāmus*
> *vocābimus*
> *vocāvimus*
> *vocāverāmus*
> *vocāverimus*

  2. moneō—third person, singular
> *monet*
> *monēbat*
> *monēbit*
> *monuit*
> *monuerat*
> *monuerit*

  3. prohibeō—second person, plural
> *prohibētis*
> *prohibēbātis*
> *prohibēbitis*
> *prohibuistis*
> *prohibuerātis*
> *prohibueritis*

  4. vocō—first person, singular
> *vocō*
> *vocābam*
> *vocābō*
> *vocāvī*
> *vocāveram*
> *vocāverō*

  5. moneō—third person, plural
> *monent*
> *monēbant*
> *monēbunt*
> *monuērunt*
> *monuerant*
> *monuerint*

6. prohibeō—second person, singular
   prohibēs
   prohibēbās
   prohibēbis
   prohibuistī
   prohibuerās
   prohibueris

J. List all the English words you can think of which come from this lesson's vocabulary words.

   1. facilitate   6. similitude
   2. fortify   7. similarity
   3. brief   8. omnipotence
   4. accelerate   9. omniscience
   5. gravity   10. omnipresence

K. Answer the following questions.

   1. What is the ablative plural form of *vīnum*? *The form is "vīnīs."*
   2. How many conjugations are there? *There are four.*
   3. What is nominative plural ending for the First Declension? *The ending is -ae.*
   4. In what things must an adjective match a noun it modifies? *An adjective must match in gender, number, and case.*
   5. List three uses of the ablative case. *Ablative of manner, ablative of means, ablative of separation.*
   6. What is the third principal part for the verb *moneō*? *The Third Principle Part is "monuī."*
   7. What is the accusative singular ending for a Third Declension Neuter adjective? *The ending is -e.*
   8. What is the dative singular ending for a Third Declension masculine adjective? *The ending is -ī.*
   9. What is the accusative plural masculine form of the word *gravis*? *The form is "gravēs."*
   10. What is the dative singular feminine form of the word *celer*? *The form is "celerī."*

READING THREE

VIR, LEO, ET SAGITTA

Vir in collēs cum arcū vēnit. Omnia animālia praeter leōnem cucurrērunt. Leō pugnāre mansit. Sed vir leōnem sagittā ferīvit et dīxit, "Sagitta meus nūntius est. Cognōsce nūntium, tum veniam."

Leō currere incēpit, sed vulpes dīxit, "Es fortis. Manē."

Leō respondit, "Numquam mihi persuadēbis. Nūntius virī horrendus est. Virum nōn convenīre cupiō."

Morum praecepta (moral): Verbum unum ad sapientem satis est.

A man went into the hills with (his) bow. All the animals ran except the lion. The lion stayed to fight. But the man shot (struck, hit) the lion with an arrow and said, "The arrow is my messenger. Recognize the messenger, then I will come."

The lion began to run, but the wolf said, "Be brave. Stay."

The lion responded, " You will never persuade me. The messenger of the man is terrible. I do not want to meet the man."

Moral: A word to the wise is sufficient.

EXERCISE TWENTY-ONE

A. Spell out in English how each Latin word should be pronounced and place the accent properly.

1. regēbāmus		re gay BAH mus
2. regēbant		re GAY bant
3. regēbātis		re gay BAH tis
4. regit		RE git
5. regunt		RE gunt
6. regimus		RE gi mus
7. rēxī		RAYKS ee
8. rēxērunt		rayks AY runt
9. rēxerit		RAYKS e rit
10. rēxerimus		rayks E ri mus

B. Chant each of the following paradigms ten times through.

ō, s, t! mus, tis, nt!
bam, bās, bat! bāmus, bātis, bant!
bō, bis, bit! bimus, bitis, bunt!
a, ae, ae, am, ā! ae, ārum, īs, ās, īs!
us, ī, ō, um, ō! ī, ōrum, īs, ōs, īs!
um, ī, ō, um, ō! a, ōrum, īs, a, īs!
sum, es, est! sumus, estis, sunt!
eram, erās, erat! erāmus, erātis, erant!
erō, eris, erit! erimus, eritis, erunt!
ī, istī, it! imus, istis, ērunt!
eram, erās, erat! erāmus, erātis, erant!
erō, eris, erit! erimus, eritis, erint!
is, is, ī, em, e! ēs, um, ibus, ēs, ibus!

C. Write the four principal parts of the following verbs. Then chant each verb "set" ten times through.

navigō, *navigō, navigāre, navigāvī, navigātum*
iaceō, *iaceō, iacēre, iacuī, - - - -*
dēfendō, *dēfendō, dēfendere, dēfendī, dēfensum*

dīcō, *dīcō, dīcere, dīxī, dictum*
dūcō, *dūcō, dūcere, dūxī, ductum*

D. Decline:

magnus agricola, *magnī agricolae, magnō agricolae, magnum agricolam, magnō agricolā, magnī agricolae, magnōrum agricolārum, magnīs agricolīs, magnōs agricolās, magnīs agricolīs*

leō fortis, *leōnis fortis, leōnī fortī, leōnem fortem, leōne fortī, leōnēs fortēs, leōnum fortium, leōnibus fortibus, leōnēs fortēs, leōnibus fortibus*

Challenge:

mare ācre, *maris ācris, marī ācrī, mare ācre, marī ācrī, maria ācria, marium ācrium, maribus ācribus, maria ācria, maribus ācribus*

E. Translate the following review sentences.

1. Puellam spectābāmus. *We were looking at the girl.*
2. Puellās et nautam laudābant. *They were praising the girls and sailor.*
3. Poēta et fēminae Deum laudābant. *The poet and women were praising God.*
4. Agricolae puellās spectant. *The farmers look at the girls.*
5. Fēminae nōn sumus. *We are not women.*
6. Agricola nōn est. *He is not a farmer.*
7. Ambulāte! *Walk!*
8. Fēminae puellam vocāvērunt. *The women called the girl.*
9. Dōnum magnum spectābunt. *They will look at the great gift.*
10. Christus Fīlius Deī est. *Christ is the Son of God.*

F. Translate the following English into Latin.

1. The brave king will lead the legions. *Rēx fortis legiōnēs dūcet.*
2. The brave son had recognized the king. *Fīlius fortis rēgem cognōverat.*
3. The mothers told the sons of the evil king about the danger. *Mātrēs fīliōs rēgis malī dē perīculō dīxerant.*
4. The Son of God ruled the grave king. *Fīlius Deī rēgem gravem rēxit.*
5. God will defeat all evil sons of evil mothers. *Deus fīliōs omnēs malārum mātrum vincet.*
6. The swift son will leave the women behind. *Fīlius celer fēminās relinquet.*
7. The woman's son sent the scout into town. *Fīlius fēminae explōrātōrem in oppidum mīsit.*
8. Evil kings did not recognize the laws of God. *Rēgēs malī lēgēs Deī nōn cognōvērunt.*
9. The law of God will not defend evil sons. *Lēx Deī fīliōs malōs nōn dēfendet.*
10. The laws of God do not rule all women. *Lēgēs Deī fēminās omnēs nōn regunt.*

G. Translate the following Latin into English.

1. Rēgem fortem vincimus. *We conquer the brave king.*
2. Rēx rēxit. *The king ruled.*
3. Māter gravis fīlium relinquit. *The serious mother leaves behind the son.*
4. Pater vīnum pōnit. *Father places the wine.*

5. Rēx oppidum dēfenderit. *The king will have defended the town.*
6. Lēx Deī bonum fīlium dūxit. *The law of God led the good son.*
7. Lēx Deī rēgem vincit. *The law of God conquers the king.*
8. Cognōvērunt montem omnem. *They recognized each mountain.*
9. Māter servōs mīserat. *The mother had sent the slaves.*
10. Servī surrēxerint. *The slaves will have risen.*

H. Give a synopsis of the following verbs.

1. dīcō—first person, plural
   dīcimus
   dīcēbāmus
   dīcēmus
   dīximus
   dīxerāmus
   dīxerimus

2. cognōscō—third person, singular
   cognōscit
   cognōscēbat
   cognōscet
   cognōvit
   cognōverat
   cognōverit

3. vincō—second person, plural
   vincitis
   vincēbātis
   vincētis
   vīcistis
   vīcerātis
   vīceritis

4. surgō—first person, singular
   surgō
   surgēbam
   surgam
   surrēxī
   surrēxeram
   surrēxerō

5. relinquō—third person, plural
   relinquunt
   relinquēbant
   relinquent
   relīquērunt
   relīquerant
   relīquerint

6. regō—second person, singular
 regis
 regēbās
 regēs
 rēxistī
 rēxerās
 rēxeris

I. List all the English words you can think of which come from this lesson's vocabulary words.

1. defend	6. dictate
2. defensive	7. dictum
3. duke	8. recognize
4. missile	9. surge
5. resurrection	10. invincible

J. Answer the following questions.
 1. What are the case endings for the First Declension? *They are* a, ae, ae, am, ā, ae, ārum, īs, ās, īs.
 2. What are the case endings for the Second Declension? *They are* us, ī, ō, um, ō, ī, ōrum, īs, ōs, īs.
 3. What are the case endings for the Third Declension? *They are* is, is, ī, em, ē, ēs, um, ibus, ēs, ibus.
 4. What are the case endings for the Second Declension Neuter? *They are* um, ī, ō, um, ō, a, ōrum, īs, a, īs.
 5. What are the conjugational endings for the imperfect tense, First Conjugation? *They are* bam, bās, bat, bāmus, bātis, bant.
 6. What is the third principal part for the verb *pōnō*? *The Third Principal Part is* "posuī."
 7. To which conjugation does *dūcō* belong? *It belongs to the Third Conjugation.*
 8. To which conjugation does *ambulō* belong? *It belongs to the First Conjugation.*
 9. To which conjugation does *mittō* belong? *It belongs to the Third Conjugation.*
 10. What is the second principal part for the verb *surgō*? *The Second Principal Part is* "surgere."

Exercise Twenty-Two

A. Spell out in English how each Latin word should be pronounced and place the accent properly.

1. faciēmus	fa ki AY mus
2. faciam	FA ki am
3. facit	FA kit
4. faciunt	FA ki unt
5. fēcistī	fay KIS tee
6. fēcerimus	fay KE ri mus

7. fēcī	FAY kee
8. cōnficere	kohn FIK e re
9. cōnfectum	kohn FEK tum
10. cupīvī	ku PEE wee

B. Chant each of the following paradigms ten times through.

ō, s, t! mus, tis, nt!

bam, bās, bat! bāmus, bātis, bant!

bō, bis, bit! bimus, bitis, bunt!

a, ae, ae, am, ā! ae, ārum, īs, ās, īs!

us, ī, ō, um, ō! ī, ōrum, īs, ōs, īs!

um, ī, ō, um, ō! a, ōrum, īs, a, īs!

sum, es, est! sumus, estis, sunt!

eram, erās, erat! erāmus, erātis, erant!

erō, eris, erit! erimus, eritis, erunt!

ī, istī, it! imus, istis, ērunt!

eram, erās, erat! erāmus, erātis, erant!

erō, eris, erit! erimus, eritis, erint!

is, is, ī, em, e! ēs, um, ibus, ēs, ibus!

C. Write the four principal parts of the following verbs. Then chant each verb "set" ten times through.

oppugnō, *oppugnō, oppugnāre, oppugnāvī, oppugnātum*

impendō, *impendō, impendēre, impendī, impensum*

cognōscō, *cognōscō, cognōscere, cognōvī, cognitum*

mittō, *mittō, mittere, mīsī, mīsum*

accipiō, *accipiō, accipere, accēpī, acceptum*

D. Decline:

parvum antrum, *parvī antrī, parvō antrō, parvum antrum, parvō antrō, parva antra, parvōrum antrōrum, parvīs antrīs, parva antra, parvīs antrīs*

flōs novus, *flōris novī, flōrī novō, flōrem novum, flōre novō, flōrēs novī, flōrum novōrum, flōribus novīs, flōrēs novōs, flōribus novīs*

Challenge:

lītus breve, *lītoris brevis, lītorī brevī, lītus breve, lītore brevī, lītora brevia, lītorum brevium, lītoribus brevibus, lītora brevia, lītoribus brevibus*

E. Translate the following review sentences.

1. Agricolae nōn sumus. *We are not farmers.*
2. Dōnum est. *It is a gift.*
3. Fēminae Deum laudābant. *The women were praising God.*
4. Deus Fīlium dabat. *God was giving the Son.*

5. Poētae cōnsilium dant. *The poets give advice.*

6. Nauta et puella fēminam amābant. *The sailor and girl were loving the woman.*

7. Laudāte! *Praise!*

8. Amāveratne Deus mundum? *Had God loved the world?*

9. Nōnne dederat cōnsilium? *He had given advice, hadn't he?*

10. Vocāverintne fēminae et puellae? *Will the women and girls have called?*

F. Translate the following English into Latin.

1. The brave king accepts the gift. *Rēx fortis dōnum accipit.*

2. The brave sons didn't kill the king, did they? *Num fīliī fortēs rēgem interfēcērunt?*

3. Did the mother receive the sons of the evil king. *Accēpitne māter fīliōs rēgis malī?*

4. The grave king will finish the plan. *Rēx gravis cōnsilium cōnficiet.*

5. He desires to have a sword. *Gladium habēre cupit.*

6. The women begin to shout. *Fēminae clāmāre incipiunt.*

7. They killed all the men in the evil city. *Virōs omnēs in malā urbe interfēcērunt.*

8. Evil kings did not receive the laws of God. *Rēgēs malī lēgēs Deī nōn accēpērunt.*

9. We do not always want the law of God. *Lēgem Deī semper nōn cupimus.*

10. The king accepted the gift of the faithful sons. *Rēx dōnum fīliōrum fīdōrum accēpit.*

G. Translate the following Latin into English.

1. Rēgem fortem interficit. *He kills the brave king.*

2. Cōnsilium fēcī. *I made a plan.*

3. Māter gravis cōnsilium accipit. *The serious mother receives advice.*

4. Pater vīnum accēpit. *Father received wine.*

5. Fīliōs fortēs habēre cupīvit. *He desired to have brave sons.*

6. Incipiō. *I begin.*

7. Incēpimus. *We began.*

8. Cōnfēcerat. *He had finished.*

9. Māter servōs accēpit. *Mother received the slaves.*

10. Servī interfēcērunt. *The slaves killed.*

H. The following sentences give the Roman explanation of how man became acquainted with fire. Translate them into English.

1. Promētheus (a Roman god) incolās terrae fēcit. *Prometheus made the inhabitants of earth.*

2. Incolae in antrīs obscūrīs et in villīs gelidīs habitāvērunt. *The inhabitants lived in dark caves and cold farmhouses.*

3. Promētheus incolās amāvit et dīxit, "Ignem ad incolās terrae dē Olympō cupiō portāre." *Prometheus loved the inhabitants of the earth and he said, "I wish to carry fire to the inhabitants of the earth from Olympus."*

4. Nocte obscūrā Promētheus ignem cēpit et ignem cum incolīs terrae posuit. *In the dark night (During the dark night) Prometheus seized fire and placed the fire with the inhabitants of earth.*

5. Incolae terrae bonum dōnum magnō cum gaudiō accēpērunt et mox multae flammae clārae in terrā calēbant. *The inhabitants of earth accepted the good gift with great joy and soon many bright flames were glowing on earth.*

I. Give a synopsis of the following verbs.

    1. facio—first person, plural
       facimus
       faciēbāmus
       faciēmus
       fēcimus
       fēcerāmus
       fēcerimus

    2. accipio—third person, singular
       accipit
       accipiēbat
       accipiet
       accēpit
       accēperat
       accēperit

    3. interficio—second person, plural
       interficitis
       interficiēbatis
       interficiētis
       interfēcistis
       interfēcerātis
       interfēceritis

    4. incipio—first person, singular
       incipiō
       incipiēbam
       incipiam
       incēpi
       incēperam
       incēperō

    5. cupio—third person, plural
       cupiunt
       cupiēbant
       cupient
       cupīvērunt
       cupīverant
       cupīverint

    6. conficio—second person, singular
       cōnficis
       cōnficiēbās
       cōnficiēs
       cōnfēcistī
       cōnfēcerās
       cōnfēceris

J. List all the English words you can think of which come from this lesson's vocabulary words.

1. concupisence
2. Cupid
3. incipient
4. accept
5. acceptance
6. confectionary

K. Answer the following questions.

1. What are the conjugational endings for the present tense, First Conjugation? *They are ō, s, t, mus, tis, nt.*
2. What are the conjugational endings for the future tense, Second Conjugation? *They are bō, bis, bit, bimus, bitis, bunt.*
3. What are the conjugational endings for the future tense, Third Conjugation? *They are m, ēs, et, ēmus, ētis, ent.*
4. What is the dative plural ending for the First Declension? *The ending is -īs.*
5. What is the genitive singular ending for the Second Declension? *The ending is -ī.*
6. What is the third principal part for the verb *interficiō*? *The Third Principal Part is "interfēcī."*
7. To which conjugation does *vincō* belong? *It belongs to the Third Conjugation.*
8. To which conjugation does *mittō* belong? *It belongs to the Third Conjugation.*
9. To which conjugation does *dēfendō* belong? *It belongs to the Third Conjugation.*
10. What is the second principal part for the verb *ambulō*? *The Second Principal Part is "ambulāre."*

READING FOUR

GEN. 1:1-10

In principiō creāvit Deus caelum et terram. Terra autem erat inānis et vacua, et tenebrae erant super faciem abyssī, et Spiritus Dei [movēbat] super aquās. Dīxitque Deus: Es lūx. Et [erat] lūx. Et vīdit Deus lūcem. [Lūx erat] bona: et dīvīsit lūcem ā tenebrīs. Appellāvit lūcem Diem, et tenebrās Noctem: [et erat] vespere et māne, diēs unus. Dīxit quoque Deus: [Es] firmāmentum in mediō aquārum: et dīvīde aquās ab aquīs. Et fēcit Deus firmāmentum, dīvīsitque aquās, quae erant sub firmamentō, ab hīs, quae erant super firmāmentum. Et [erat] ita. Vocāvitque Deus firmāmentum, Caelum: et [erat] vespere et māne, diēs secundus. Dīxit vērō Deus: [Congregāte] aquae, quae sub caelō sunt, in locum unum: et [appārē] arida. Et [erat] ita. Et vocāvit Deus aridam Terram, congregātiōnēsque aquārum appellāvit Maria. Et vīdit Deus [omnia]. [Omnia erat] bonum.

[Teacher's Note: As the English translation via the Latin is twice removed from the original language, it is sometimes difficult to match a direct-from-Hebrew account. Nevertheless, searching for the author's intended meaning by studying word order, vocabulary choice, and case use is a worthy exercise and will bear fruit in the thoughtful student's English composition as well as in his future Latin work. At this point in his studies, the student should be able to grasp much of the content of the reading without doing a verbatim translation of each line.]

In the beginning God created the sky and the land. However, the land was formless and empty, and shadows were over the face of the abyss, and the Spirit of God was moving over the waters. And God said, "Be light." And there was light. And God saw the light. The light was good: and He divided the light from the shadows. He called the light Day, and the shadows Night: and there was evening and morning, day one. And God also said: "Be a support in the middle of the waters: and divide the waters from the waters." And God made a support, and He divided waters, which were below the support, from those, which were above the support. And it was thus. And God called the support Sky: and there was evening and morning, the second day. And truly God said, "Gather, waters which are under the sky, into one place: and appear, dry land." And it was thus. And God called the dry land Earth, and the gathering of waters He called Seas. And God saw everything. Everything was good.

Exercise Twenty-Three

A. Spell out in English how each Latin word should be pronounced and place the accent properly.

1. manūs		MA noos
2. manibus		MA ni bus
3. manū		MA noo
4. adventum		ad WEN tum
5. adventibus		ad WEN ti bus
6. adventuī		ad WEN tu ee
7. manuum		MA nu um
8. casuum		KA su um
9. exitibus		ex I ti bus
10. impetibus		im PE ti bus

B. Chant each of the following paradigms five times through, beginning at the bottom and chanting you way to the top!

ō, s, t! mus, tis, nt!
bam, bās, bat! bāmus, bātis, bant!
bō, bis, bit! bimus, bitis, bunt!
a, ae, ae, am, ā! ae, ārum, īs, ās, īs!
us, ī, ō, um, ō! ī, ōrum, īs, ōs, īs!
um, ī, ō, um, ō! a, ōrum, īs, a, īs!
sum, es, est! sumus, estis, sunt!

eram, erās, erat! erāmus, erātis, erant!
erō, eris, erit! erimus, eritis, erunt!
ī, istī, it! imus, istis, ērunt!
eram, erās, erat! erāmus, erātis, erant!
erō, eris, erit! erimus, eritis, erint!
is, is, ī, em, e! ēs, um, ibus, ēs, ibus!
us, ūs, uī, um, ū! ūs, uum, ibus, ūs, ibus!

C. Write the four principal parts of the following verbs. Then chant each verb "set" ten times through.

portō, *portō, portāre, portāvī, portātum*
moneō, *moneō, monēre, monuī, monitum*
maneō, *maneō, manēre, mansī, mansum*
dēfendō, *dēfendō, dēfendī, dēfensum*
capiō, *capiō, capere, cēpī, captum*

D. Decline:

līberī meī, *līberōrum meōrum, līberīs meīs, līberōs meōs, līberīs meīs*

[Teacher's Note: The nominative and genitive adjectives here are masculine, even if a woman is speaking because the adjective agrees with the noun it modifies in gender, number, and case. Children is a collective noun, plural only, and always masculine.]

omnis bōs, *omnis bovis, omnī bovī, omnem bovem, omnī bove, omnēs bovēs, omnium bovum, omnibus bovibus, omnēs bovēs, omnibus bovibus*

coniunx similis, *coniugis similis, coniugī similī, coniugem similem, coniuge similī, coniugēs similēs, coniugum similium, coniugibus similibus, coniugēs similēs, coniugibus similibus*

Challenge:

adulēscēns celer, *adulēscentis celeris, adulēscentī celerī, adulēscentem celerem, adulēscente celerī, adulēscentēs celerēs, adulēscentium celerium, adulēscentibus celeribus, adulēscentēs celerēs, adulēscentibus celeribus*

E. Translate the following review sentences.

1. Agricolae et nautae nōn sumus. *We are not farmers and sailors.*
2. Dōnum bonum est. *It is a good gift.*
3. Fēmina Deum laudābit. *The woman will praise God.*
4. Deus Fīlium dedit. *God gave the Son.*
5. Poēta cōnsilium bonum dat. *The poet gives good advice.*
6. Nautae et puellae fēminās amābunt. *The sailors and girls will love the women.*
7. Spectāte! *Look!*
8. Amāverantne mundum? *Had they loved the world?*
9. Nōnne dederant cōnsilium malum? *They had given bad advice, hadn't they?*
10. Spectāverintne fēminae et puellae? *Will the women and girls have looked?*

F. Translate the following English into Latin.

    1. The brave king praises the attack. *Rēx fortis impetum laudat.*

    2. The mother does not want misfortune. *Māter casum nōn cupit.*

    3. The woman accepted the arrival of the evil king. *Fēmina adventum rēgis malī accēpit.*

    4. The farmer recognized the house. *Agricola domum cognōvit.*

    5. He desires a swift departure. *Exitum celerem cupit.*

    6. The women saw the arrival of the army. *Fēminae adventum exercitūs vīdit.*

    7. They led the attack. *Impetum dūxērunt.*

    8. We saw the hand of God. *Manum Deī vīdimus.*

    9. The law of God is not misfortune. *Lēx Deī casus nōn est.*

    10. The king defended the port of the high city. *Rēx portum urbis altae dēfendit.*

G. Translate the following Latin into English.

    1. Rēgis fortis impetum laudāvit. *He praised the attack of the brave king.*

    2. Fēminae adventum spectant. *The women look at the arrival.*

    3. Māter gravis domum accipit. *The serious mother receives the house.*

    4. Pater manum agricolae accēpit. *Father accepted the hand of the farmer.*

    5. Casum cupīvit. *He desired misfortune.*

    6. Impetum cupīvit. *He desired the attack.*

    7. Exitum rēgis spectāmus. *We look at the departure of the king.*

    8. Rēx impetum laudābit. *The king will praise the attack.*

    9. Māter servōs domūs accēpit. *The mother received the slaves of the house.*

    10. Servī casum spectāvērunt. *The slaves looked at the misfortune.*

H. Give a synopsis of the following verbs.

    1. faciō—second person, plural

        facitis

        faciēbātis

        faciētis

        fēcistis

        fēcerātis

        fēceritis

    2. accipiō—first person, singular

        accipiō

        accipiēbam

        accipiam

        accēpī

        accēperam

        accēperō

3. interficiō—third person, plural
  interficiunt
  interficiēbant
  interficient
  interfēcērunt
  interfēcerant
  interfēcerint
4. incipiō—second person, singular
  incipis
  incipiēbās
  incipiēs
  incēpistī
  incēperās
  incēperis
5. cupiō—first person, plural
  cupimus
  cupiēbāmus
  cupiēmus
  cupīvimus
  cupīverāmus
  cupīverimus
6. cōnficiō—third person, singular
  cōnficit
  cōnficiēbat
  cōnficiet
  cōnfēcit
  cōnfēcerat
  cōnfēcerit

I. List all the English words you can think of which come from this lesson's vocabulary words.

1. impetuous   6. casualty
2. impetus
3. adventure
4. exit
5. domicile

J. Answer the following questions.

1. How many conjugations are there? *There are four.*
2. How many declensions are there? *There are five.*
3. What is the genitive singular ending for *rēx*? *The form is "rēgis."*
4. What is the dative plural ending for *agricola*? *The form is "agricolīs."*
5. What is the genitive singular ending for the Second Declension? *The ending is -ī.*
6. What are the case endings for the Fourth Declension? *They are* us, ūs, uī, um, ū, ūs, uum, ibus, ūs, ibus.

7. What are the case endings for the Fourth Declension Neuter? *They are ū, ūs, ū, ū, ū, ua, uum, ibus, ua, ibus.*

8. What is apposition? *It is when one noun stands alongside another one to explain more about it.*

9. What is the predicate nominative? *It is a noun in the predicate which takes the nominative case because of the verb "is."*

10. What case does the preposition *ad* take? *It takes the accusative.*

EXERCISE TWENTY-FOUR

A. Spell out in English how each Latin word should be pronounced and place the accent properly.

1. audīre	ow DEE re
2. invenīre	in we NEE re
3. ventum	WEN tum
4. dormiō	DOR mi oh
5. perveniō	per WE ni oh
6. dormītum	dor MEE tum
7. impedīvī	im pe DEE wee
8. pervēnī	per WAY nee
9. pervēnit	per WAY nit
10. impedīverint	im pe DEE we rint

B. Chant each of the following paradigms two times through.

ō, s, t! mus, tis, nt!

bam, bās, bat! bāmus, bātis, bant!

bō, bis, bit! bimus, bitis, bunt!

a, ae, ae, am, ā! ae, ārum, īs, ās, īs!

us, ī, ō, um, ō! ī, ōrum, īs, ōs, īs!

um, ī, ō, um, ō! a, ōrum, īs, a, īs!

sum, es, est! sumus, estis, sunt!

eram, erās, erat! erāmus, erātis, erant!

erō, eris, erit! erimus, eritis, erunt!

ī, istī, it! imus, istis, ērunt!

eram, erās, erat! erāmus, erātis, erant!

erō, eris, erit! erimus, eritis, erint!

C. Chant each of the following paradigms ten times through.

is, is, ī, em, e! ēs, um, ibus, ēs, ibus!

us, ūs, uī, um, ū! ūs, uum, ibus, ūs, ibus!

D. Write the four principal parts of the following verbs. Then chant each verb "set" ten times through.

audiō, *audiō, audīre, audīvī, audītum*
inveniō, *inveniō, invenīre, invēnī, inventum*
veniō, *veniō, venīre, vēnī, ventum*
impediō, *impediō, impedīre, impedīvī, impedītum*
dormiō, *dormiō, dormīre, dormīvī, dormītum*

E. Decline:

dux līber, *ducis līberī, ducī līberō, ducem līberum, duce līberō, ducēs līberī, ducum līberōrum, ducibus līberīs, ducēs līberōs, ducibus līberīs*

magna laus, *magnae laudis, magnae laudī, magnam laudem, magnā laude, magnae laudēs, magnārum laudum, magnīs laudibus, magnās laudēs, magnīs laudibus*

arcus tuus, *arcūs tuī, arcuī tuō, arcum tuum, arcū tuō, arcūs tuī, arcuum tuōrum, arcibus tuīs, arcūs tuōs, arcibus tuīs*

[Teacher's Note: *Arcus* is from the Reading Three vocabulary list.]

Challenge:

exitus celer, *exitūs celeris, exituī celerī, exitum celerem, exitū celerī, exitūs celerēs, exituum celerium, exitibus celeribus, exitūs celerēs, exitibus celeribus*

F. Translate the following review sentences.

1. Rēgem fortem interficit. *He kills the brave king.*
2. Cōnsilium fēcī. *I made a plan.*
3. Māter gravis cōnsilium accipit. *The serious mother receives advice.*
4. Pater vīnum accēpit. *Father received wine.*
5. Fīliōs fortēs habēre cupīvit. *He desired to have brave sons.*
6. Incipiō. *I begin.*
7. Incēpimus. *We began.*
8. Cōnfēcerat. *He had finished.*
9. Māter servōs accēpit. *Mother received the slaves.*
10. Servī interfēcērunt. *The slaves killed.*

G. Translate the following English into Latin.

1. The short woman hears the law of God. *Fēmina breve lēgem Deī audit.*
2. The mother comes upon the easy road. *Māter viam facilem invenit.*
3. The woman hinders the arrival of the fierce king. *Fēmina adventum regis acris (ferī) impedit.*
4. The swift farmer arrives. *Agricola celer pervenit.*
5. The tired poets sleep. *Poētae dēfessī dormiunt.*
6. All the women come and see. *Fēminae omnēs veniunt et vident.*
7. They heard the fierce attack. *Impetum acrem (ferum) audīvērunt.*
8. Soon they assembled. *Mox convēnērunt.*

9. Then we arrived. *Tum pervēnimus.*

10. The king hindered the attack of the brave sons. *Rēx impetum filiōrum fortium impedīvit.*

H. Translate the following Latin into English.

1. Adulēscēns regem audīvit. *The youth heard the king.*
2. Carmen avium audiō. *I hear the song of the birds.*
3. Canis acer dormit. *The fierce dog sleeps.*
4. Mōns fīlium impedit. *The mountain hinders the son.*
5. Cum navibus pervenīmus. *We arrive with the ships.*
6. Custōs dormīvit. *The watchman slept.*
7. Prope fontem conveniūmus. *We assemble near the fountain.*
8. Hospes iuvenēs audit. *The guest hears the youth (pl.).*
9. Dux leōnēs pugnat. *The leader fights the lions.*
10. Viam brevem invēnistis. *You came upon the short road.*

I. Give a synopsis of the following verbs.

1. audiō—second person, plural
   audītis
   audiēbātis
   audiētis
   audīvistis
   audīverātis
   audīveritis
2. inveniō—first person, singular
   inveniō
   inveniēbam
   inveniam
   invēnī
   invēneram
   invēnerō
3. veniō—third person, plural
   veniunt
   veniēbant
   venient
   vēnērunt
   vēnerant
   vēnerint
4. impediō—second person, singular
   impedīs
   impediēbās
   impediēs
   impedīvistī
   impedīverās
   impedīveris

5. dormiō—first person, plural
  dormīmus
  dormiēbāmus
  dormiēmus
  dormīvimus
  dormīverāmus
  dormīverimus
6. conveniō—third person, singular
  convenit
  conveniēbat
  conveniet
  convēnit
  convēnerat
  convēnerit

J. List all the English words you can think of which come from this lesson's vocabulary words.

1. auditorium
2. invent
3. invention
4. dormitory
5. convention
6. convene
7. impediment
8. audible
9. audit
10. impede

K. Answer the following questions.

1. What are the case endings for the Third Declension? *The endings are* is, is, ī, em, e, ēs, um, ibus, ēs, ibus.
2. What are the case endings for the Fourth Declension? *The endings are* us, ūs, uī, um, ū, ūs, uum, ibus, ūs, ibus.
3. What is the genitive plural ending for *rēx*? *The form is* "rēgum."
4. What is the accusative plural ending for *manus*? *The form is* "manūs."
5. What is the Second Principal Part of *audiō*? *The Second Principal Part is* "audīre."
6. What is the distinctive ending of Fourth Conjugation verbs? *The distinctive ending is the* -ūs *of the genitive singular.*
7. What is the Second Principal Part of *dormiō*? *The Second Principal Part is* "dormīre."
8. What case does *ad* take? *It takes the accusative.*
9. What case does *prope* take? *It takes the accusative.*
10. What is the infinitive of *dormiō*? *The infinitive is* "dormīre."

EXERCISE TWENTY-FIVE

A. Spell out in English how each Latin word should be pronounced and place the accent properly.

1. diēs	DI ays
2. diem	DI em
3. rēs	rays
4. spēī	SPAY ee
5. meridiem	me RI di em
6. diērum	di AY rum
7. diēbus	di AY bus
8. diē	DI ay
9. rēī	RAY ee
10. rem	rem

B. Chant each of the following paradigms two times through.

ō, s, t! mus, tis, nt!
bam, bās, bat! bāmus, bātis, bant!
bō, bis, bit! bimus, bitis, bunt!
a, ae, ae, am, ā! ae, ārum, īs, ās, īs!
us, ī, ō, um, ō! ī, ōrum, īs, ōs, īs!
um, ī, ō, um, ō! a, ōrum, īs, a, īs!
sum, es, est! sumus, estis, sunt!
eram, erās, erat! erāmus, erātis, erant!
erō, eris, erit! erimus, eritis, erunt!

C. Chant each of the following paradigms ten times through.

ī, istī, it! imus, istis, ērunt!
eram, erās, erat! erāmus, erātis, erant!
erō, eris, erit! erimus, eritis, erint!
is, is, ī, em, e! ēs, um, ibus, ēs, ibus!
us, ūs, uī, um, ū! ūs, uum, ibus, ūs, ibus!
ēs, ēī, ēī, em, ē! ēs, ērum, ēbus, ēs, ēbus!
rēs, rēī, rēī, rem, rē! rēs, rērum, rēbus, rēs, rēbus!

D. Write the four principal parts of the following verbs. Then chant each verb "set" ten times through.

laudō, *laudō, laudāre, laudāvī, laudātum*
spectō, *spectō, spectāre, spectāvī, spectātum*
inveniō, *inveniō, invenīre, invēnī, inventum*
perveniō, *perveniō, pervenīre, pervēnī, perventum*
habeō, *habeō, habēre, habuī, habitum*
videō, *videō, vidēre, vīdī, vīsum*

E. Decline:

puella pulchra, *puellae pulchrae, puellae pulchrae, puellam pulchram, puellā pulchrā, puellae pulchrae, puellārum pulchrārum, puellīs pulchrīs, puellās pulchrās, puellīs pulchrīs*

bellum horrendum, *bellī horrendī, bellō horrendō, bellum horrendum, bellō horrendō, bella horrenda, bellōrum horrendōrum, bellīs horrendīs, bella horrenda, bellīs horrendīs*

lūx clara, *lūcis clarae, lūcī clarae, lūcem claram, lūce clarā, lūcēs clarae, lūcum clarārum, lūcibus clarīs, lūcēs clarās, lūcibus clarīs*

Challenge:

manus gravis, *manūs gravis, manuī gravī, manum gravem, manū gravī, manūs gravēs, manuum gravium, manibus gravibus, manūs gravēs, manibus gravibus*

F. Translate the following review sentences.

1. Fēminam audīvit. *He heard the woman.*
2. Fēminās audiō. *I hear the women.*
3. Deus nōn dormit. *God does not sleep.*
4. Deus puellās audit. *God hears the girls.*
5. Agricolae oppidum inveniunt. *The farmers come upon the town.*
6. Dormīvēruntne puellae? *Did the girls sleep?*
7. Rēx impetum laudābat. *The king was praising the attack.*
8. Nautae casum spectant. *The sailors look at the misfortune.*
9. Puellae et agricolae domum spectābunt. *The girls and farmers will look at the house.*
10. Adventum rēgis spectāmus. *We look at the arrival of the king.*

G. Translate the following English into Latin.

1. The woman hears (her) husband. *Fēmina coniugem audit.*
2. The scout comes upon the lions. *Explōrātor leōnēs invenit.*
3. The women hinder the arrival of the maiden. *Fēminae adventum virginis impediunt.*
4. The weary farmer arrived with a burden. *Agricola cum onere pervēnit.*
5. The grateful poets slept under the roof. *Poētae gratī sub tectum dormīvērunt.*
6. The women came and saw the lofty tower. *Fēminae turrim arduam vēnērunt et vīdērunt.*
7. The king heard the attack of the ship. *Rēx impetum navis audīvit.*
8. Often they assembled in the thick forest. *Saepe in silvā densā convēnērunt.*
9. Soon we arrived at the mouth of the river. *Mox ad ōs fluminis pervēnimus.*
10. The faithful king hinders the attack of the fierce sons. *Rēx fīdus impetum fīliōrum ferōrum (acrium) impedit.*

H. Translate the following Latin into English.

1. Rēx spem habet. *The king has hope.*
2. Rem fēminārum audiō. *I hear the thing (matter) of the women.*
3. Pater dormīvit. *The father slept.*
4. Pater impetum impedīvit. *The father hindered the attack.*

5. Dormīvimus. *We slept.*
6. Diēs pervenit. *Day arrives.*
7. Convēnistis. *You assembled.*
8. Rēx famam iuvenis audit. *The king hears the story of the youth.*
9. Fīlius canem audit. *The son hears the dog.*
10. Longam viam invēnistī. *You came upon the long road.*

I. Give a synopsis of the following verbs.

1. laudō—second person, plural
    laudātis
    laudābātis
    laudābitis
    laudāvistis
    laudāverātis
    laudāveritis
2. spectō—first person, singular
    spectō
    spectābam
    spectābō
    spectāvī
    spectāveram
    spectāverō
3. inveniō—third person, plural
    inveniunt
    inveniēbant
    invenient
    invēnērunt
    invēnerant
    invēnerint
4. perveniō—second person, singular
    pervenīs
    perveniēbās
    perveniēs
    pervēnistī
    pervēnerās
    pervēneris
5. habeō—first person, plural
    habēmus
    habēbāmus
    habēbimus
    habuimus
    habuerāmus
    habuerimus

6. videō—third person, singular

videt

vidēbat

vidēbit

vīdit

vīderat

vīderit

J. List all the English words you can think of which come from this lesson's vocabulary words.

1. republic
2. face
3. facial

K. Answer the following questions.

1. What case is used for the subject of a sentence? *The nominative case is used.*
2. What case is used for the direct object of a sentence? *The accusative case is used.*
3. What case is used for the indirect object of a sentence? *The dative case is used.*
4. What case is used to show possession? *The genitive case is used.*
5. What case is used to show means? *The ablative case is used.*
6. What case is used to show accompaniment? *The ablative case is used.*
7. What is the accusative plural of *spēs*? *The form is "spēs."*
8. What is the dative plural of *rēs*? *The form is "rēbus."*
9. What are the case endings of the Fifth Declension? *The endings are ēs, ēī, ēī, em, ē, ēs, ērum, ēbus, ēs, ēbus.*
10. What are the case endings of the Fourth Declension? *The endings are us, ūs, uī, um, ū, ūs, uum, ibus, ūs, ibus.*

EXERCISE TWENTY-SIX

A. Spell out in English how each Latin word should be pronounced and place the accent properly.

1. hōrum	HOH rum
2. hārum	HAH rum
3. haec	hyke
4. hōc	hohk
5. huius	HUI us
6. huic	huik
7. illīus	il LEE us
8. illōrum	il LOH rum
9. illud	IL lud
10. illī	IL lee

B. Chant each of the following paradigms ten times through.

is, is, ī, em, e! ēs, um, ibus, ēs, ibus!

us, ūs, uī, um, ū! ūs, uum, ibus, ūs, ibus!

ēs, ēī, ēī, em, ē! ēs, ērum, ēbus, ēs, ēbus!

hic, haec, hoc! huius, huius, huius! huic, huic, huic! hunc, hanc, hoc! hōc, hāc, hōc!

hī, hae, haec! hōrum, hārum, hōrum! hīs, hīs, hīs! hōs, hās, haec! hīs, hīs, hīs!

ille, illa, illud! illīus, illīus, illīus! illī, illī, illī! illum, illam, illud! illō, illā, illō!

illī, illae, illa! illōrum, illārum, illōrum! illīs, illīs, illīs! illōs, illās, illa! illīs, illīs, illīs!

is, ea, id! eius, eius, eius! eī, eī, eī! eum, eam, id! eō, eā, eō!

eī, eae, ea! eōrum, eārum, eōrum! eīs, eīs, eīs! eōs, eās, ea! eīs, eīs, eīs!

C. Write the four principal parts of the following verbs. Then chant each verb "set" ten times through.

videō, *vidēre, vīdī, vīsum*

faciō, *facere, fēcī, factum*

cupiō, *cupīre, cupīvī, cupītum*

incipiō, *incipere, incēpī, inceptum*

interficiō, *interficere, interfēcī, interfectum*

moneō, *monēre, monuī, monitum*

D. Decline:

is puer, *eius puerī, eī puerō, eum puerum, eō puerō, eī puerī, eōrum puerōrum, eīs puerīs, eōs*
    puerōs, eīs puerīs

illa famula, *illīus famulae, illī famulae, illam famulam, illā famulā, illae famulae, illārum famulārum,*
    illīs famulīs, illās famulās, illīs famulīs

hoc onus, *huius oneris, huic onerī, hoc onus, hōc onere, haec onera, hōrum onerum, hīs oneribus,*
    haec onera, hīs oneribus

E. Translate the following review sentences.

1. Agricolae et nautae Deum audīvērunt. *The farmers and sailors heard God.*
2. Dōna bona dant. *They give good gifts.*
3. Fēminae audient. *The women will hear.*
4. Fīlius pervenit. *The son arrives.*
5. Fēminae convēnērunt. *The women assembled.*
6. Puellae fēminās audient. *The girls will hear the women.*
7. Poēta Deum invenit. *The poet finds God.*
8. Pervēnī. *I arrived.*
9. Puellae et agricolae ad oppidum ambulābant. *The girls and farmers were walking into town.*
10. Fēminae et puellae dormīverant. *The women and girls had slept.*

F. Translate the following English into Latin.

1. This woman hears the law of God. *Haec fēmina lēgem Deī audit.*
2. That mother comes upon this road. *Illa māter hanc viam invenit.*
3. The woman hinders the arrival of this king. *Fēmina adventum huius rēgis impedit.*
4. These farmers arrive. *Hī agricolae perveniunt.*
5. These poets sleep, but those poets always labor. *Hī poētae dormiunt, sed illī poētae semper laborant.*
6. Those women come and see. *Illae fēminae veniunt et vident.*
7. They heard this attack. *Hunc impetum audīvērunt.*
8. This king heard that attack. *Hic rēx illum impetum audīvit.*
9. These poets saw that girl. *Hī poētae illam puellam vīdērunt.*
10. This woman hindered that man. *Haec fēmina illum virum impedīvit.*

Use *is, ea, id* for the following translations.

11. This horse is running in the field. *Is equus in agrō currunt.*
12. That man overcomes the horse. *Is vir equum vincit.*
13. Did you see those swift birds? *Vīdisne eās avēs celerēs?*
14. Why are these tired watchmen standing in the river? *Cūr eī custōdēs dēfessī in flumine stant?*
15. Those men have fought a long war. *Eī virī longum bellum pungnāvērunt.*

G. Translate the following Latin into English.

1. Illum rēgem audīvit. *He heard that king.*
2. Illās fēminās audiō. *I hear those women.*
3. Haec māter gravis dormit. *This serious mother sleeps.*
4. Hic pater fīlium impedit. *This father hinders the son.*
5. Hī poētae illās puellās spectant. *These poets look at those girls.*
6. Hic agricola dormīvit. *This farmer slept.*
7. Ille rēx Deum laudāvit. *That king praised God.*
8. Illae fēminae audient. *Those women will hear.*
9. Māter illōs servōs audit. *The mother hears those slaves.*
10. Illam viam invēnistis. *You came upon that road.*

   [Teacher's Note: In the following sentences, *this*, *that* and *these*, *those* are interchangeable in these translations without context.]

11. Is Deus auctōritātem patrī dedit. *This God gave authority to the father.*
12. Deus eam auctōritātem matrī dabat. *God was giving that authority to the mother.*
13. Flōrem in eā mensā posuit. *She placed the flower on that table.*
14. Eī agricolae in pulchrīs villīs habitant. *Those farmers live in beautiful villas (farmhouses).*
15. Pulchrae villae prope eam brevem viam sunt. *The beautiful villas are near that short way (street, road).*

H. Give a synopsis of the following verbs.

1. videō—second person, plural
   vidētis
   vidēbātis
   vidēbitis
   vīdistis
   vīderātis
   vīderitis

2. faciō—first person, singular
   faciō
   faciēbam
   faciam
   fēcī
   fēceram
   fēcerō

3. cupiō—third person, plural
   cupiunt
   cupiēbant
   cupient
   cupīvērunt
   cupīverant
   cupīverint

4. incipiō—second person, singular
   incipis
   incipiēbas
   incipiēs
   incēpistī
   incēperās
   incēperis

5. interficiō—first person, plural
   interficimus
   interficiēbāmus
   interficiēmus
   interfēcimus
   interfēcerāmus
   interfēcerimus

6. moneō—third person, singular
   monet
   monēbat
   monēbit
   monuit
   monuerat
   monuerit

I. Answer the following questions.

1. What are the case endings for the Third Declension? *The endings are* is, is, ī, em, e, ēs, um, ibus, ēs, ibus.

2. What are the case endings for the Fourth Declension? *The endings are* us, ūs, uī, um, ū, ūs, uum, ibus, ūs, ibus.

3. What are the case endings for the Fifth Declension? *The endings are* ēs, ēī, ēī, em, ē, ēs, ērum, ēbus, ēs, ēbus.

4. What is the accusative plural ending for *rēs*? *The form is* "rēs."

5. What is the Second Principal Part of *perveniō*? *The Second Principal Part is* "pervenīre."

6. What is the way to say *that* if it points to a masculine noun in the accusative case? *The form is* "illum."

7. What is the way to say *these* if it points to a feminine noun in the dative case? *The form is* "hīs."

8. What is the way to say *those* if it points to a neuter noun in the ablative case? *The form is* "illīs."

9. What is the way to say *this* if it points to a masculine noun in the nominative case? *The form is* "hic."

10. What is the way to say *that* if it points to a feminine noun in the accusative case? *The form is* "illam."

EXERCISE TWENTY-SEVEN

A. Spell out in English how each Latin word should be pronounced and place the accent properly.

1. eōrum		e OH rum
2. eārum		e AH rum
3. eī		E ee
4. illud		IL lud
5. eius		E yus
6. eō		E oh
7. eōs		E ohs
8. illōrum		il LOH rum

B. Chant each of the following paradigms ten times through.

is, is, ī, em, e! ēs, um, ibus, ēs, ibus!

us, ūs, uī, um, ū! ūs, uum, ibus, ūs, ibus!

ēs, ēī, ēī, em, ē! ēs, ērum, ēbus, ēs, ēbus!

hic, haec, hoc! huius, huius, huius! huic, huic, huic! hunc, hanc, hoc! hōc, hāc, hōc!

hī, hae, haec! hōrum, hārum, hōrum! hīs, hīs, hīs! hōs, hās, haec! hīs, hīs, hīs!

ille, illa, illud! illīus, illīus, illīus! illī, illī, illī! illum, illam, illud! illō, illā, illō!

illī, illae, illa! illōrum, illārum, illōrum! illīs, illīs, illīs! illōs, illās, illa! illīs, illīs, illīs!

is, ea, id! eius, eius, eius! eī, eī, eī! eum, eam, id! eō, eā, eō!

eī, eae, ea! eōrum, eārum, eōrum! eīs, eīs, eīs! eōs, eās, ea! eīs, eīs, eīs!

C. Write the four principal parts of the following verbs. Then chant each verb "set" ten times through.

maneō, *manēre, mānsī, mānsum*
capiō, *capere, cēpī, captum*
feriō, *ferīre, ferīvī, ferītum*
currō, *currere, cucurrī, cursum*
mittō, *mittere, mīsī, missum*
respondeō, *respondēre, respondī, responsum*

D. Decline:

is canis, *eius canis, eī canī, eum canem, eō cane, eī canēs, eōrum canium, eīs canibus, eōs canēs, eīs canibus*

illa lēx, *illīus lēgis, illī lēgī, illam lēgem, illā lēge, illae lēgēs, illārum lēgum, illīs lēgibus, illās lēgēs, illīs lēgibus*

hoc mare, *huius maris, huic marī, hoc mare, hōc marī, haec maria, hōrum marium, hīs maribus, haec maria, hīs maribus*

E. Translate the following review sentences.

1. Rēx spem habet. *The king has hope.*
2. Rem fēminārum audiō. *I hear the thing (matter) of the women.*
3. Pater dormīvit. *The father slept.*
4. Pater impetum impedīvit. *The father hindered the attack.*
5. Dormīvimus. *We slept.*
6. Diēs pervenit. *Day arrives.*
7. Convēnistis. *You assembled.*
8. Rēx famam iuvenis audit. *The king hears the story of the youth.*
9. Fīlius canem audit. *The son hears the dog.*
10. Longam viam invēnistī. *You came upon the long road.*

F. Translate the following English into Latin.

1. This woman hears the law of God, that one does not hear it. *Haec fēmina lēgem Deī audit, illa eam nōn audit.*
2. That mother comes upon this road, but she does not walk on it. *Illa māter hanc viam invenit, sed illa in eā nōn ambulat.*
3. The woman hinders the arrival of this king and she does not love him. *Fēmina adventum huius rēgis impedit et ea hunc nōn amat.*
4. These farmers arrive. Do those arrive? *Hī agricolae perveniunt. Perveniuntne illōs?*
5. These poets sleep, but those always labor. *Hī poētae dormiunt, sed illī semper laborant.*
6. Those women come and see, but they do not work. *Illae fēminae veniunt et vident, sed eae nōn laborant.*
7. They heard this attack, but it was not serious. *Hunc impetum audīvērunt, sed is nōn gravis erat.*

8. This king heard that attack and he went to fight. *Hic rēx illum impetum audīvit et hic (is) pugnāre vēnit.*
9. These poets saw that girl, but she did not see them. *Hī poētae illam puellam vīdērunt, sed ea (illa) hōs nōn vīdit.*
10. This woman hindered that man and sent him to the island. *Haec fēmina illum virum impedīvit et eum mīsit ad īnsulam.*
11. This horse is running in the field with him. *Hic equus in agrō cum eī currunt.*
12. He overcomes the horse. *Is equum vincit. (Equum vincit.)*
13. Did you see those swift birds and did you hear them? *Vīdisne eās avēs celerēs et eās audīvistis?*
14. Why are they (these tired watchmen) standing in the river? *Cūr eī in flūmine stant?*
15. Those men have fought a long war and they have fought it with sharp arrows. *Eī virī longum bellum pugnāvērunt et eī (cum) sagittīs acribus id pugnāvērunt.*

G. Translate the following Latin into English. The words in ( ) are for referral only. Do not translate them.

> [Teacher's Note: As the translations become more complex because of more options for pronoun choice, it may be necessary to check individual students' work for correct variations from the responses given.]

1. Illum (rēgem) audīvit. *He heard that one.*
2. Illās (fēminās) audiō. *I hear those.*
3. Haec (māter gravis) dormit. *This one (this woman) sleeps.*
4. Hic (pater) fīlium impedit. *This one (this man) hinders the son.*
5. Hī (poētae) illās (puellās) spectant. *These (men) look at those (women).*
6. Hic (agricola) dormīvit. *This one (man) slept.*
7. Ille (rēx) Deum laudāvit. *That one (man) praised God.*
8. Illae (fēminae) audient. *Those (women) will hear.*
9. Māter illōs (servōs) audit. *The mother hears those (men).*
10. Illam (viam) invēnistis. *You came upon that (one).*
11. Is (Deus) auctōritātem patrī dedit. *He gave the father authority. (He gave to the father the authority.)*
12. Deus eam (auctōritātem) mātrī dabat. *God was giving that (it) to the mother.*
13. Flōrem in eā (mēnsā) posuit. *She placed the flower on it.*
14. Eī (agricolae) in pulchrīs villīs habitant. *Those (They) live in beautiful villas (farmhouses).*
15. Eae (Pulchrae villae) prope eam brevem viam sunt. *They are near that short way (street, road).*

H. Give a synopsis of the following verbs.

1. maneō—second person, plural
   manētis
   manēbātis
   manēbitis
   mānsistis
   mānserātis
   mānseritis

2. capiō—first person, singular
   capiō
   capiēbam
   capiam
   cēpī
   cēperam
   cēperō

3. feriō—third person, plural
   ferit
   feriēbat
   feriet
   ferīvit
   ferīverat
   ferīverit

4. currō—second person, singular
   curris
   currēbās
   curret
   cucurristī
   cucurrerās
   cucurreris

5. mittō—first person, plural
   mittimus
   mittēbāmus
   mittēmus
   mīsimus
   mīserāmus
   mīserimus

6. respondeō—third person, singular
   respondet
   respondēbat
   respondēbit
   respondit
   responderat
   responderit

I. Answer the following questions.

   1. What are the case endings for the Third Declension? *The endings are* is, is, ī, em, e, ēs, um, ibus, ēs, ibus.

   2. What are the case endings for the Fourth Declension? *The endings are* us, ūs, uī, um, ū, ūs, uum, ibus, ūs, ibus.

   3. What are the case endings for the Fifth Declension? *The endings are* ēs, ēī, ēī, em, ē, ēs, ērum, ēbus, ēs, ēbus.

4. What is the accusative plural ending for *rēs*? *The form is* "rēs."

5. What is the Second Principal Part of *perveniō*? *The Second Principal Part is* "pervenīre."

6. What is the way to say *that* if it refers to a masculine noun in the accusative case? *The form is* "illum."

7. What is the way to say *these* if it refers to a feminine noun in the dative case? *The form is* "hīs."

8. What is the way to say *those* if it refers to a neuter noun in the ablative case? *The form is* "illīs."

9. What is the way to say *this* if it refers to a masculine noun in the nominative case? *The form is* "hic."

10. What is the way to say *that* if it refers to a feminine noun in the accusative case? *The form is* "illam."

EXERCISE TWENTY-EIGHT

A. Spell out in English how each Latin word should be pronounced and place the accent properly.

1. quī		kwee
2. quae		kweye
3. quod		kwod
4. cuius		KU yus
5. cui		KU ee

B. Chant each of the following paradigms ten times through.

is, is, ī, em, e! ēs, um, ibus, ēs, ibus!

us, ūs, uī, um, ū! ūs, uum, ibus, ūs, ibus!

ēs, ēī, ēī, em, ē! ēs, ērum, ēbus, ēs, ēbus!

hic, haec, hoc! huius, huius, huius! huic, huic, huic! hunc, hanc, hoc! hōc, hāc, hōc!

hī, hae, haec! hōrum, hārum, hōrum! hīs, hīs, hīs! hōs, hās, haec! hīs, hīs, hīs!

ille, illa, illud! illīus, illīus, illīus! illī, illī, illī! illum, illam, illud! illō, illā, illō!

illī, illae, illa! illōrum, illārum, illōrum! illīs, illīs, illīs! illōs, illās, illa! illīs, illīs, illīs!

is, ea, id! eius, eius, eius! eī, eī, eī! eum, eam, id! eō, eā, eō!

eī, eae, ea! eōrum, eārum, eōrum! eīs, eīs, eīs! eōs, eās, ea! eīs, eīs, eīs!

quī, quae, quod! cuius, cuius, cuius!, cui, cui, cui! quem, quam, quod! quō, quā, quō!

quī, quae, quae! quōrum, quārum, quōrum! quīs, quīs, quīs! quōs, quās, quae! quibus, quibus, quibus!

C. Write the four principal parts of the following verbs. Then chant each verb "set" ten times through.

rogō, *rogāre, rogāvī, rogātum*

maneō, *manēre, mānsī, mānsum*

moneō, *monēre, monuī, monitum*

habeō, *habēre, habuī, habitum*

dīcō, *dīcere, dīxī, dictum*

mittō, *mittere, mīsī, missum*

D. Decline:

magnus canis, *magnī canis, magnō canī, magnum canem, magnō cane, magnī canēs, magnōrum canium, magnīs canibus, magnōs canēs, magnīs canibus*

longa lēx, *longae lēgis, longae lēgī, longam legem, longā lege, longae lēgēs, longārum lēgum, longīs lēgibus, longās lēgēs, longīs lēgibus*

mare quiētum, *maris quiētī, marī quiētō, mare quiētum, marī quiētō, maria quiēta, marium quiētōrum, maribus quiētīs, maria quiēta, maribus quiētīs*

E. Translate the following review sentences.

1. Hic (agricola) dormīvit. *This one (man) slept.*
2. Ille (rēx) Deum laudāvit. *That one (man) praised God.*
3. Illae (fēminae) audient. *Those (women) will hear.*
4. Māter illōs (servōs) audit. *The mother hears those (men).*
5. Illam (viam) invēnistis. *You came upon that (one).*
6. Is (Deus) auctōritātem patrī dedit. *He gave the father authority. (He gave to the father the authority.)*
7. Deus eam (auctōritātem) matrī dabat. *God was giving that (it) to the mother.*
8. Florem in eā (mensā) posuit. *She placed the flower on it.*
9. Eī (agricolae) in pulchrīs villīs habitant. *Those (They) live in beautiful villas (farmhouses).*
10. Eae (Pulchrae villae) prope eam brevem viam sunt. *They are near that short way (street, road).*

F. Translate the following English into Latin.

1. This woman who hears the law of God does not love it. *Haec fēmina quae lēgem Deī audit eam nōn amat.*
2. That mother who comes upon this road walks on it. *Illa māter quae hanc viam invenit in eā ambulat.*
3. The woman who hinders the arrival of this king does not love him. *Fēmina quae adventum huius rēgis impedit et ea hunc nōn amat.*
4. These farmers who are working in the fields arrive. *Hī agricolae, quī in agrōs labōrant, perveniunt.*
5. These poets who do not always labor sleep. *Hī poētae dormiunt quī nōn semper labōrant.*
6. Those women whom they watched did not carry burdens. *Illae fēminae quās spectāvērunt onerum nōn portāvērunt.*
7. They heard this attack which was not serious. *Hunc impetum audīvērunt quem nōn gravis erat.*
8. This king heard the army which he went to fight. *Hic rēx exercitum audīvit quem pugnāre vēnit.*
9. These poets saw the girl, who did not see them. *Hī poētae puellam vīdērunt, quae hōs nōn vīdit.*
10. The woman who hindered that man sent him to the island. *Fēmina quae illum virum impedīvit eum mīsit ad īnsulam.*

G. Read the following passage. As you read, follow these five commands:

1) Underline each relative pronoun and circle its antecedent. Draw an arrow to show the relationship.

2) Tell the case and the reason for that case for each relative pronoun.

3) Put an X on all the adjectives which modify feminine nouns.

4) Draw a box around all the verbs in the perfect tense.

5) Double underline the imperative verbs. (They give a command.)

VIR QUI NON EST TREPIDUS

Olim rēx Babylōnicus cum Isrāēlītīs pugnāvit, quōs facile vīcit. Deinde ad rēgiam paucōs puerōs Isrāēlītārum captīvōs dūxit, inter quōs erat Daniēl.

Daniēlī, quī propter sapientiam ēgregius erat, rēx dedit multa praemia et multōs honōrēs.

Sociī rēgis autem, quī invidiōsī erant, dīxērunt, "O rēx, Daniēl neque deōs Babylōnicōs neque tē ipsum, rēgem huius terrae, adōrat. Lēge Babylōnicā Daniēl perīre dēbet."

Propter haec verba sociōrum, rēx miserrimus Daniēlem in spēluncam ubi erant multī leōnēs iēcit.

Daniēl autem nōn erat territus; clāmāvit, "Deus quem adōrō mē servābit!"

Rēx dīxit, "Es fīdus, Daniēl; deus tuus, quem semper adōrās, tē servābit."

Postrīdiē rēx māne ad spēluncam properāvit et magnā vōce Daniēlem vocāvit, "O, Daniēl, servāvitne tē deus quem adōrās?"

Ex spēluncā Daniēl respondit, "O rēx, angelus vēnit, quī apud mē in hāc spēluncā mānsit. Leōnēs mē nōn vulnerāvērunt. Deus mē servāvit!"

Tum rēx populō dīxit, "Studium et scientia et sapientia sunt in hōc virō. Deus quī Daniēlem servāvit deus vērus est. Capite illōs quī eum accūsāvērunt! Illōs iacite in eandem spēluncam ubi leōnēs sunt!"

TRANSLATION:
Once the king of Babylon fought with the Israelites, whom he conquered easily. Then he led to the palace a few captive boys of the Isrealites, among whom was Daniel.

To Daniel, who was outstanding because of his wisdom, the king gave many rewards and many honors. Friends of the king, however, who were jealous, said, "Oh king, Daniel neither worships the Babylonian gods nor you yourself, king of this earth. By Babylonian law Daniel ought to perish."

Because of these words of his friends, the most wretched king threw Daniel into a cave where there were many lions.

However, Daniel was not afraid; he shouted, "God, whom I worship will save me."

The king said, "Be faithful, Daniel; your god, whom you always worship, will save you."

The next day in the morning the king hurried to the cave and called Daniel with a loud voice, "Oh, Daniel, did the god whom you worship save you?"

From the cave Daniel responded, "Oh king, an angel came, who stayed with me in this cave. The lions did not hurt me. God saved me!"

Then the king said to the people, "Zeal, knowledge, and wisdom are in this man. God who saved Daniel is the true God. Seize those who accused him! Throw them into the same cave where the lions are!"

H. Give a synopsis of the following verbs.

1. audiō—second person, plural
   audītis
   audiēbātis
   audiētis
   audīvistis
   audīverātis
   audīveritis

2. inveniō—first person, singular
   inveniō
   inveniēbam
   inveniam
   invēnī
   invēneram
   invēnerō

3. veniō—third person, plural
   veniunt
   veniēbant
   venient
   vēnērunt
   vēnerant
   vēnerint

4. impediō—second person, singular
   impedīs
   impediēbās
   impediēs
   impedīvistī
   impedīverās
   impedīveris

5. dormiō—first person, plural
   dormīmus
   dormiēbāmus
   dormiēmus
   dormīvimus
   dormīverāmus
   dormīverimus

6. conveniō—third person, singular
   convenit
   conveniēbat
   conveniet
   convēnit
   convēnerat
   convēnerit

I. Answer the following questions.

1. What are the case endings for the Third Declension? *The endings are is, is, ī, em, e, ēs, um, ibus, ēs, ibus.*

2. What are the case endings for the Fourth Declension? *The endings are us, ūs, uī, um, ū, ūs, uum, ibus, ūs, ibus.*

3. What are the case endings for the Fifth Declension? *The endings are ēs, ēī, ēī, em, ē, ēs, ērum, ēbus, ēs, ēbus.*

4. What is the accusative plural ending for *manus*? *The form is* "manūs."

5. What is the Second Principal Part of *ambulō*? *The Second Principal Part is* "ambulāre."

6. What is the way to say *that* if it modifies a masculine noun in the accusative case? *The form is* "illum."

7. What is the way to say *these* if it refers to a feminine noun in the dative case? *The form is* "hīs."

8. What is the way to say *those* if it modifies a neuter noun in the ablative case? *The form is* "illīs."

9. What is the way to say *this* if it refers to a masculine noun in the nominative case? *The form is* "hic."

10. What is the way to say *that* if it modifies a feminine noun in the accusative case? *The form is* "illam."

EXERCISE TWENTY-NINE

A. Spell out in English how each Latin word should be pronounced and place the accent properly. Then translate each form.

1. portor	POR tor	I am carried
2. vocābāris	woh cah BAH ris	you were called
3. vidēbitur	wi DAY bi tur	he will be seen
4. capientur	ca pi EN tur	they will be seized
5. audīminī	ou DEE mi nee	you are seen

B. Chant each of the following paradigms ten times through.

is, is, ī, em, e! ēs, um, ibus, ēs, ibus!

us, ūs, uī, um, ū! ūs, uum, ibus, ūs, ibus!

ēs, ēī, ēī, em, ē! ēs, ērum, ēbus, ēs, ēbus!

hic, haec, hoc! huius, huius, huius! huic, huic, huic! hunc, hanc, hoc! hōc, hāc, hōc!

hī, hae, haec! hōrum, hārum, hōrum! hīs, hīs, hīs! hōs, hās, haec! hīs, hīs, hīs!

ille, illa, illud! illīus, illīus, illīus! illī, illī, illī! illum, illam, illud! illō, illā, illō!

illī, illae, illa! illōrum, illārum, illōrum! illīs, illīs, illīs! illōs, illās, illa! illīs, illīs, illīs!

is, ea, id! eius, eius, eius! eī, eī, eī! eum, eam, id! eō, eā, eō!

eī, eae, ea! eōrum, eārum, eōrum! eīs, eīs, eīs! eōs, eās, ea! eīs, eīs, eīs!

quī, quae, quod! cuius, cuius, cuius! cui, cui, cui! quem, quam, quod! quō, quā, quō!

quī, quae, quae! quōrum, quārum, quōrum1 quīs, quīs, quīs! quōs, quās, quae! quibus, quibus, quibus!

r, ris, tur! mur, minī, ntur!

C. Write the four principal parts of the following verbs. Then chant each verb "set" ten times through.

cupiō, *cupīre, cupīvī, cupītum*
faciō, *facere, fēcī, factum*
feriō, *ferīre, ferīvī, ferītum*
dūcō, *dūcere, dūxī, dūctum*
veniō, *venīre, vēnī, ventum*

D. Decline:

bōs novus, *bovis novī, bovī novō, bovem novum, bove novō, bovēs novī, bovum novōrum, bovibus novīs, bovēs novōs, bovibus novīs*

arbor ūmida, *arboris ūmidae, arborī ūmidae, arborem ūmidam, arbore ūmidā, arborēs ūmidae, arborum ūmidārum, arboribus ūmidīs, arborēs ūmidās, arboribus ūmidīs*

carmen grātum, *carminis grātī, carminī grātō, carmen grātum, carmine grātō, carmina grāta, carminum grātōrum, carminibus grātīs, carmina grāta, carminibus grātīs*

Challenge:

cursus celeris, *cursūs celeris, cursuī celerī, cursum celerem, cursū celerī, cursūs celerēs, cursuum celerium, cursibus celeribus, cursūs celerēs, cursibus celeribus*

rēs facilis, *rēī facilis, rēī facilī, rem facilem, rē facilī, rēs facilēs, rērum facilium, rēbus facilibus, rēs facilēs, rēbus facilibus*

E. Translate the following English into Latin.
1. I was carried from the building. *Ab aedificiō portābar.*
2. You were seen by God. *A Deō vidēbāris.*
3. He will be held by the fierce youth. *Ab adulēscente ferō habēbitur.*
4. We haven't been frightened by the tired lions. *Nōn territī sumus ā leōnibus dēfessīs.*
5. You (pl.) had been filled with good food. *Bonō cibō complētī erātis.*
6. They will have been recognized near the water. *Prope aquam cognitī erunt.*
7. I have been guided to this place. *Ad illum locum dūctus sum.*
8. She had been left behind to work in the house (domus). *Labōrāre in domū relicta erat.*
9. He will have been accepted. *Acceptus erit.*
10. You had been wished a good journey. *Bonum iter cupītus erās.*

F. Read the following passage. Give a verbatim (word by word) translation of each sentence which contains a passive verb.

ARIES AUREUS

Olim in terrā longinquā habitābant frāter et soror, Phrixus et Hellē. ¹Hī līberī autem crūdēliter (*cruelly*) vexābantur. Dī Olympī igitur frātrem sorōremque servāre (*to save*) cupiēbant.

   Mercurius in conciliō deōrum dīxit, "Hōs līberōs ex patriā ad locum tūtum portābō, sed iter perīculōsum erit."

²Frāter sororque in magnō agrō ubi ovēs erant saepe vidēbantur. ³Ab ovēs nōn vulnerābantur.

⁴Olim, autem (*however*) ariēs (*ram*) aureus inter ovēs vīsus est ā līberīs. Is ariēs nōn erat ferus. ⁵Rē vērā (*in truth*) quiētus erat, dum (*while* (with pres. tense)) corōnīs (*garlands, crowns*) adōrnātur. Tum frāter et soror in tergum (*-ī, N. back*) arietis ascendērunt (*climbed*).⁶Subitō ariēs volāre (*to fly*) incēpit, et līberī territī in caelum celeriter, (*quickly*) portābantur.

⁷Ab ariete trāns montēs, flūmina, maria volātī sunt. Tum Hellē dēfessa dē tergō arietis in mare angustum (*narrow*)cecidit. (*fell*) Phrixus tristis (*sad*) erat.

Post multās horās ariēs Phrixum tūtum (*safely*) dēposuit in Colchide, terrā cuius rēx benignus (*kind*) erat.

⁸Ibi (*there*) vōx ā Phrixō audītus est, "Sacrificā hunc arietem, sed servā vellus (-eris, N. *fleece*). Pōne vellus in arbore sacrā. ⁹Sum Mercurius; dracō (*dragon*) mittētur quī noctū et interdiū arborem spectābit." Posteā Phrixus vellus ad rēgiam (*palace*) portāvit. Rēx, ubi fābulam arietis aureī audīvit, dīxit, "Tū (*you*)eris fīlius meus. ¹⁰Vellus aureum saepe quaerētur (quaerō- *to seek, to search for*). Magnus honor ad rēgnum meum veniet."

Once in a far away land lived a brother and sister, Phrixus and Helle. These children were cruelly vexed. The gods of Olympus therefore were wanting to save the brother and sister.

Mercury said in the council of the gods, "I will carry these children from their fatherland to a safe place, but the journey will be dangerous."

The brother and sister were often seen in a large field where there were sheep. They were not harmed by the sheep.

Once, however, a golden ram has been seen by the children among the sheep. The (this) ram was not fierce. In truth, (in fact) he was quiet while he is adorned with garlands. Then the brother and sister climbed onto (his) ** back. Suddenly the ram began to fly, and the frightened children were carried quickly into the sky.*

They are flown by the ram across mountains, rivers, and seas. Then tired Helle fell from the back of the ram into a narrow sea.** Phrixux was sad.

After many hours the ram put Phrixus down safely (put down Phrixus safe) in Colchis, a land (ablative in apposition to Colchide) whose king was kind. There a voice has been heard by Phrixus, " Sacrifice this ram, but keep the fleece. Put the fleece in the sacred tree. I am Merucry' a dragon is being sent who will watch the tree by night and by day." Afterwards Phrixus carried the fleece to the palace. The king, when he heard the story of the ram, said, "You will be my son. The golden fleece is often sought. It will bring great honor to my kingdom."

¹Hī līberī autem crūdēliter vexābantur. *These children, however, were vexed cruelly.*

²Frāter sororque in magnō agrō ubi ovēs erant saepe vidēbantur. *The brother and sister were often seen in a large field where there were sheep.*

³Ab ovēs nōn vulnerābantur. *They were not harmed by the sheep.*

⁴Olim, autem ariēs aureus inter ovēs vīsus est ā līberīs. *Once, however, a golden ram was seen by the children among the sheep.*

---

*The possessive pronoun is frequently omitted in Latin when the meaning is clear without it.
** It is from this legend of Helle that we get the name Hellespont, also called the Dardanelles.

⁵Rē vērā quiētus erat, dum corōnīs adōrnātur. *In truth he was quiet, (calm) while he is being adorned with garlands.*

⁶Subitō ariēs volāre incēpit, et līberī territī in caelum celeriter portābantur. *Suddenly, the ram began to fly, and the frightened children were carried quickly into the sky.*

⁷Ab ariete trāns montēs, flūmina, maria volātī sunt. *They are flown by the ram across mountains, rivers, and seas.*

⁸Ibi vōx ā Phrixō audītus est, "Sacrificā hunc arietem, sed servā vellus." *There a voice is heard by Phrixus, "Sacrifice this ram, but keep the fleece."*

⁹Sum Mercurius; dracō mittētur quī noctū et interdiū arborem spectābit. *I am Mercury; a dragon is being sent who will watch the tree by night and by day.*

¹⁰Vellus aureum saepe quaerētur. *The golden fleece is often sought.*

I. Give a synopsis of the following verbs *in the passive voice.*

1. mutō—second person, plural
   mutāminī
   mutābāminī
   mutābiminī
   mutātī estis
   mutātī erātis
   mutātī eritis

2. habeō—first person, singular
   habeor
   habēbar
   habēbor
   habitus sum
   habitus eram
   habitus erō

3. veniō—third person, plural
   veniuntur
   veniēbantur
   venientur
   ventī sunt
   ventī erant
   ventī erunt

4. impediō—second person, singular
   impedīris
   impediēbāris
   impediēris
   impedītus es
   impedītus erās
   impedītus eris

5. dīcō—first person, plural

dīcimur

dīcēbāmur

dīcēmur

dīctī sumus

dīctī erāmus

dīctī erimus

6. conveniō—third person, singular

convenītur

conveniēbātur

conveniētur

conventus est

conventus erat

conventus erit

J. Answer the following questions.

1. What are the present system, passive voice, verb endings? *r, ris, tur! mur, minī, ntur!*

2. What are the case endings for the First Declension? *a, ae, ae, am, ā! ae, ārum, īs, ās, īs!*

3. What are the case endings for the Second Declension? *us, ī, ō, um, ō! ī, ōrum īs, ōs, īs!*

4. What is the accusative plural ending for *ovis*? *The ending is -ēs (ovēs)*

5. What is the Second Principal Part of *impediō*? *The Second Principal Part is* impedīre.

6. How many conjugations are there? *There are four conjugations.*

7. How many declensions are there? *There are five declensions.*

8. What is apposition? *It is when one noun stands alongside another one to explain more about it.*

9. What is the predicate nominative? *It is a noun in the predicate which takes the nominative case because of the verb "is."*

10. What case does the preposition *aa* take? *It takes the accusative.*

NOTES

NOTES

NOTES